E-LEARNING DEPARTMENT OF ONE

EMILY WOOD

atd
PRESS

ATD Press is an internationally renowned source of insightful and practical information on talent development, training, and professional development.

ATD Press
1640 King Street
Alexandria, VA 22314 USA

Ordering information: Books published by ATD Press can be purchased by visiting ATD's website at www.td.org/books or by calling 800.628.2783 or 703.683.8100.

Library of Congress Control Number: 2018958852
ISBN-10: 1-947308-82-3
ISBN-13: 978-1-947308-82-4
e-ISBN: 978-1-947308-83-1

ATD Press Editorial Staff
Director: Kristine Luecker
Manager: Melissa Jones
Community of Practice Manager, Learning Technologies: Justin Brusino
Developmental Editor: Jack Harlow
Senior Associate Editor: Caroline Coppel
Text Design: Shirley Raybuck
Cover Design: Alban Fischer, Alban Fischer Design

Printed by Versa Press, East Peoria, IL

To Jonathan for inspiring me.
To Brian for keeping me sane.
To Christopher for pushing me.

Contents

Foreword

I met Emily because she shares my commitment to lifelong learning and development.

Within just a few months of connecting with her, I knew that she was the real deal. With more than 14 years of experience in training and instructional design, she has executed in-person and online training programs for the federal government, nonprofits, and the corporate sector. Market research, management, scrum, social media, training: There's nothing Emily can't do.

This is why when she asked me to write the foreword for this book, I immediately said yes. I knew exactly why she wrote it and why she'd asked me, the founder of the eLearning Industry network, to offer my insight into this topic.

More professionals are choosing to go it alone in the e-learning marketplace. It's not easy to be a department of one in any area, let alone online learning, where the instructional designer, e-learning developer, graphic designer, multimedia expert, client service coordinator, editor, course tester, and project manager are the same person.

Being a soloist comes with a lot of responsibilities and requires a lot of creativity and flexibility, an independent mind, and great organizational skills. I know a few individuals who fit this description and they produce outstanding work, even though it seems to outsiders as if the work just magically gets done. That's not the case. These professionals are truly exceptional in preparing, organizing, planning, implementing, tracking, budgeting and, more often than not, thinking out of the box.

The good news is, these skills are ones you can learn. And that's where this book comes in. It's filled with incredibly valuable information and resources for those who are about to expand their horizons and take on multiple e-learning roles.

As you can probably guess, the tips and best practices written here work. Otherwise I wouldn't be endorsing Emily as strongly as I am.

The best thing about this book is that it's written in a way that shows respect for your time. The author knows your time is valuable, so she's presented the information in such a way that you can jump to the chapter that interests you, if you know your gaps and want to focus on a specific area. On the other hand, if you're new to e-learning and don't know where to start, the chapter order will walk you through the process.

Chapter 1 focuses on organizational needs assessment. If you join an organization for the first time or move into a training and development role, then this chapter will be extremely valuable to you, helping you get to know your company and the people and processes it encompasses. How are you going to get information about the staff for whom you will be designing e-learning? What questions do you need to ask to learn more about the technology you'll be using? How are you going to choose the right project management style? Will you have the opportunity to review the work created or purchased before you started? What about the evaluation data you have access to?

After you're done with your company's needs assessment, it's time to assess organizational and individual employee needs for specific training modules, which brings us to chapter 2. Here you'll learn how to determine needs and gaps and build the solution to move learners to the desired state. Knowing the organization, learners, and expectations for training will allow you to establish what qualifies as success and ensure that all stakeholders (including subject matter experts and whoever will approve the final deliverable) understand the timeline.

This is, of course, impossible without good project management, about which you'll learn in chapter 3. If you despise wasting time with bureaucracy, the tips provided here will help you not only ensure you deliver usable content in a timely manner, but also estimate the amount of time you spend on each project for assessing costs and ROI (not to mention transitioning between projects when you need a mental break).

Chapter 4 is all about your favorite frenemy, subject matter experts, or SMEs—unless, of course, you're the subject matter expert in your project! Although SMEs are invaluable to the content development process, they're often either unavailable or unable to understand how long it will take you to code the training content into the module. In this chapter, you'll learn how to cultivate a positive, trusting working relationship with your SME and be more creative in your development.

In chapter 5, you'll learn how to identify the right learning approach by taking into consideration the stakeholders for the module being created and the availability of the content, as well as how to collaborate with others, design a curriculum for your learning solution, determine its length, select technology, and create emotional connections to your content.

In chapter 6, you'll find out why creating a storyboard is critical—regardless of the project management approach you take—and how it will save you development time in the long run.

Chapters 7 to 10 are all about specific activities, techniques, and tools for creating engaging material. From branching scenarios to simulations, games, interactions, and feedback; from choosing the right authoring tool to selecting the right learning management system; from appropriate uses of audio to creating video and graphics in e-learning—in these four chapters, you'll find some of the best e-learning development tips you've read in a long, long time.

And what about accessibility? Even if you don't need to make your content accessible, is it worth ensuring that your future learners will be able to take your course if they need accessibility features? It certainly is. In chapter 11, you'll find some great hacks for accessibility development and making sure that your content is accessible to all.

Chapter 12 focuses on testing. It contains everything you need to know about alpha testing with SMEs, beta testing quality control, and getting feedback from alpha and beta tests to ensure a smooth implementation.

Now that the module is published and the learners are taking it, you can begin the assessment and evaluation process outlined in chapter 13. From knowing the difference between assessing and evaluating to avoiding analysis paralysis and evaluating yourself, in this chapter you'll discover how to determine whether you met your, and others', expectations for your project.

Finally, chapter 14 is a great gift for those who want to further their professional development by building on self-evaluation and continuous growth. Tools, software titles, conferences, and other resources are here to keep you motivated, especially when you're not feeling inspired.

My favorite part? The "Embracing the Reality" and "Advice From the Trenches" sidebars throughout the book. In every "Embracing the Reality" story, you'll read about another learning professional who worked in a department of one and made it happen. Similarly, in "Advice From the Trenches," you'll get the greatest tips and tricks from accomplished training professionals to make the most of working on your own. They're fantastic.

E-learning Department of One inspired me, taught me things, and made me think. If you're hungry to be the best version of yourself, grab a copy!

Christopher Pappas
Founder, eLearning Industry Network
December 2018

Introduction

Don't worry—you're not alone. Well, technically, if you picked up this book, you probably identify as an "e-learning department of one," but you aren't the only person in this situation. There are lots of us out here.

Join me in co-opting the introvert's motto: [We] Unite Separately [to Develop E-Learning].

How Did I Get Here?

From the experienced instructional designer at an organization that is just starting out with e-learning, to the experienced marketer who needs to develop an e-learning module for sales support, to a subject matter expert sharing content with a larger audience, to a classroom teacher taking subjects online, we are all at various stages of our knowledge of e-learning and training development. However, what we have in common is that we are the rare entrepreneurs who find ourselves in the position of developing it on our own.

We can see the departments-of-one trend in the proliferation of mobile devices and the increased value of just-in-time training. What could be better than having your employee access the information on how you want them to work at the exact time they're doing it on a device they already own? What better way is there for an employee to spend five minutes of time between clients than learning about a new initiative, upskilling, or refreshing knowledge from a training course they took last week?

Small organizations might hire you as a freelance or 1099 contractor, while medium-sized organizations might offer you full-time employee status. Hiring you is probably a test as to whether e-learning is feasible for the organization. With a small company, this could lead you to years of work as a freelancer or eventually being hired in-house, if that's what you'd like. For a medium or larger organization, it may lead to the development of a department.

Hopefully you're happy to have found yourself in the job that you have now. You're building the best training that you can with the time and materials that you can access. But, you might be starting to see gaps. You have found websites that show off the latest and greatest e-learning and you want to build those things, but don't know how to get there. Or, you have all the skills to do the work that you want to do, but aren't sure where to start with the giant pile of projects sitting in front of you.

I wrote this book because I found that I was acting as an instructional designer, project manager, and e-learning developer for a midsized company and wanted resources but wasn't able to find them. This book is an amalgamation of the things that I've learned and tips and tricks for development that you can now take advantage of in your e-learning development as a department of one.

How Do I Use This Book?

This book does not need to be read in the order the chapters appear. If you know where your gaps are and you want to focus on specific areas, jump directly to that. Your time is valuable! If you're new to your situation and you want to figure out where to start, these chapters are ordered in a way that will walk you through the process of developing a project and delivering it to your client.

Let's start with some assumptions:

You are a lifelong learner and you want to better yourself. This book will be a starting point for you to assess your strengths and weaknesses to build better modules.

You have expertise in one or more of the following:

- **Instructional design.** You're a teacher or an instructional designer who already knows how to develop effective training. You understand SMART goals and learning objectives. You know your audience and how to build activities that will help them understand the content. You know how to evaluate the effectiveness of training.

- **Multimedia or e-learning development.** You know the insides and outsides of a computer and have a few software titles that you use to create training that other people have written. You know your way around a microphone, a video camera, and editing software. You know how to learn more about the software titles you are using or will use to increase your proficiency.

- **Content expertise.** You've got a PhD in astrophysics and you want to show the world how the universe is expanding. You know how to do a backflip and can teach other people to do it too.

You're passionate about your content and want to put it out there.

You're doing this alone. You did pick up a book with *Department of One* in the title, after all. You have limited financial, time, and knowledge resources at your disposal to get your content out into the world.

You are developing e-learning, or something that is viewed or taken on a computer or mobile device with an Internet connection or with the ability to download materials for later access without Internet.

You know something about the audience for your content. You'll reach them by seeing them in class, working with them, selling a product to them. Maybe you're putting content on YouTube just to share your knowledge with the world to make it a better place. You have in mind the language of your learner, their level of background knowledge on the subject you're teaching, their age, the technology they'll use to access your training, and the speed of their Internet. If you don't know all of this, no worries—I'll discuss how to find the answers in chapter 1.

What's in This Book

Here is a takeaway from each chapter to give you an idea of an immediately usable idea or suggestion:

- **Chapter 1: Organizational Needs Assessment.** Whether you're a new hire brought on to design e-learning or an instructional designer asked to take it on, conduct an organizational needs assessment before you start on any projects. This will provide the preliminary information that can inform the development of all content and the overall goals for e-learning.

- **Chapter 2: Module-Specific Needs Assessment.** Each time a new module is developed, an e-learning needs assessment should be completed. Even in cases where you can reuse information from other modules, this step should not be skipped entirely.

- **Chapter 3: Project Management.** Project management is worth the time to ensure that you deliver usable content in a timely manner. It will minimize time wasted with bureaucracy by making your work transparent.

- **Chapter 4: Working With SMEs.** A positive, trusting working relationship with your subject matter expert, or SME, will allow you to be more creative in your development.

- **Chapter 5: Content Development.** There's more to "developing" content than writing it yourself. Curate from other sources, both within your organization and from outside.

- **Chapter 6: Storyboarding.** Spending time on this step will save you development time in the long run. One storyboard does not meet all needs. Customize for the instruction. ·
- **Chapter 7: Building Activities.** The best activities are the ones that allow learners to fail fast and often and get the feedback and scaffolding to be successful when confronted with the same situation in real life.
- **Chapter 8: E-Learning Authoring and Development Tools.** There are some great, free tools that you can start using today to create e-learning. No one paid tool is better than others; there are trade-offs in support, usability, and cost.
- **Chapter 9: Audio.** If you decide to use audio, whether that's a voice-over, music, or both, think about accessibility, education level, and content difficulty when choosing what can be offered as audio in your module.
- **Chapter 10: Graphics and Video.** If you want to save time when recording video, build a storyboard, write a script, and stick to it. Consider the benefits and drawbacks of purchasing graphics and video versus developing them yourself.
- **Chapter 11: Accessibility.** A growing body of legislation on accessibility for anything found online has made it easier to develop to meet a variety of needs.
- **Chapter 12: Testing and Sharing.** Having an LMS can make sharing content easier, but it isn't the only or best way for you to reach your audience.
- **Chapter 13: Assessment and Evaluation.** With xAPI, the assessment of whether an employee is able to perform the tasks taught in the module can be observed on the job and tracked.
- **Chapter 14: Resources and Professional Development.** Connecting with other e-learning departments of one will give you

the chance to give and receive advice and keep you motivated in your development, especially when you're not feeling inspired.

Each chapter features two kinds of sidebars. The first was inspired by a recent conference I attended. There, a participant demonstrated a project she'd created. When an audience member asked about a particular piece of functionality, she responded by saying that because she worked alone and had tight deadlines for publication, she'd learned to "embrace the sh*ttiness" of the work she was doing. She made things that worked but with an added a bit of humor—she referred to it as "quirky."

I agree with the idea of knowing what we can do with our available resources, but prefer a more positive spin. The stories from the people doing this work and making it happen are in sidebars called "Embracing the Reality." Some of these stories are positive, and describe projects that worked out well. Others demonstrate that being a limited resource, sometimes you have to walk away because you don't have the ability to resolve every single issue. These sidebars are intended to give you a window into the work that other professionals contend with in similar situations.

Tips to make the most of working on your own are in a sidebar called "Advice From the Trenches." In these callouts, you'll find workarounds and specific advice on how to improve your skills and knowledge in an area.

Note that for both sidebars, stories with no name attached are my own.

In each chapter, I'll provide examples to show how different content might be optimally handled. To serve as a thread throughout the book, I wanted an example that would cross all industries and organization sizes, so I've chosen new supervisor training. My hope is that even if you don't have new supervisor experience, it's a topic that you will likely deal with from either an instructional design or a learner point of view in the future. Plus, what organization couldn't use more and better new supervisor training?

I welcome you to our e-learning community of one. My sincere hope is that with this book, you choose to stay awhile.

CHAPTER 1

Organizational Needs Assessment

It's worth mentioning at this point that the definition of a "department of one" could vary depending on how your organization assigns instructional design tasks. This book encompasses quite a bit of work that might be done by an instructional designer. If the organization combines both instructional design and e-learning design and development, you might be called an e-learning developer. If your organization has a separate instructional designer and you code e-learning based on their work, your role might be referred to as an e-learning designer. Regardless of which way you work in the organization, this first chapter is valuable because it will help you get to know your organization and the people and processes it encompasses. The second chapter focuses on the instructional design aspect of individual module development and will have the most value for e-learning developers.

If you are brand-new to an organization as an e-learning developer, you'll need to do a needs assessment of your position within the organization and build relationships with the staff. If you've been with your organization but are stepping into the realm of e-learning, you may want to skim through this chapter to see if there is helpful information that you had not considered. If you are established as the e-learning developer for your organization, consider skipping ahead to chapter 2.

To begin the organizational needs assessment, you'll want to learn about the end users of your e-learning content and the experts who support the technology behind it. That starts with your company's human resources and information technology departments.

People

If your role doesn't fall within your organization's human resources department, make some friends there to get information about the staff for whom you will be designing and delivering e-learning. Start off by asking for:

- **An organizational chart or hierarchy.** Knowing where the audience is coming from will also change the content. Think about developing a management training module for warehouse staff and then doing the same training for accountants. While the content will be similar in nature, its presentation, activities, and expectations might vary. The layout of the organization will help you identify who approves content. It will also show where you fit into the organization and can help you navigate the politics around your content development.
- **Length of time with the organization.** Organizations with staff who have been there for numerous years have a completely different expectation of policies than organizations with higher turnover rates. If e-learning is new to the organization, you'll need to consider a change management process in addition to everything else you create.
- **Education level.** Discussed later in this chapter, the language level, examples, and activities should be different for an audience with seventh-grade reading skills than one with postgraduate reading skills. You'll also have higher expectations for background knowledge if the audience has a degree in that subject matter.

- **Technical savvy.** If this is your audience's first time taking a formal e-learning course, the module should look significantly different than if the target audience has already taken online courses. In addition, the modules' usability will also vary considerably by both the text size and the activity explanations.
- **Disabilities.** In a perfect world, all training would be fully accessible to anyone who chooses to take it. This book has an entire chapter dedicated to 508 compliance considerations. Because you're a department of one and the costs associated with 508-compliant development are significant, your organization may choose to limit accessibility to the disabilities presently in your workforce. The drawback to this is the amount of work you would have to do if someone with a different disability begins to work there.
- **Preferred language.** Find out if the organization has a policy on supported languages. Many organizations that support more than one language have their entire policy manual available in additional languages. If a portion of your audience speaks a specific language that your organization does not officially support, it might be worth considering localizing content to better tailor training content to them.

Embracing the Reality

Obtaining confidential information from the human resources department, particularly if you are not a member of that department, is exceptionally difficult. When you're a recent hire and the concept of e-learning is new to your organization, it may be hard for HR to understand why you'd need such detailed information to build a training program. To persuade them, try presenting them with the following scenario:

You are providing training on a subject that has been explained to you by someone else. You're onstage and the audience is in darkness; you cannot see or hear them. You don't know what they know, and you won't receive feedback from them until a month from now. How do you know that they understand what you're sharing with them?

The more information you receive about the audience now, the more effective the training will be from the start. Otherwise, feedback won't come in until after you can do user testing, revisions, and a larger-scale distribution, all of which are likely months from initial development.

Technology

The information technology, or IT, department will be indispensable to you. They will likely provide all the technical support for password resetting, the hardware you and the learners use, and, if it's not your responsibility, the administration of the learning management system (LMS). Because this might be your first interaction with IT besides when they hooked up your computer, here are some questions to consider asking that department:

- **LMS support.** Who maintains the LMS? Who builds user accounts in the LMS? Who provides training on the LMS? Who builds reports in the LMS? Who imports courses into the LMS?
- **Hardware support.** What hardware does the company provide? Are there laptops, desktops, or mobile devices? What operating systems are supported? Are you expected to develop courses for all these platforms? If a learner uses personal equipment, does IT support any issues they may have?
- **Quality assurance (QA) testing.** Will IT QA test the courses on the supported browsers and hardware?
- **Bug reporting and error logs.** How will IT share bugs, errors, and tech support information with you?
- **Training time.** Is there an expectation that staff members take training "on the clock," or can they do it anytime? If they have a deadline for a module and are doing it outside of regular company hours, what support do they have?

A Day in the Life

It will take some time to develop your first modules. If you're setting up the LMS and meeting the subject matter experts (SMEs) to start on work, this is an ideal time to shadow different members of the organization. You'll get to know what their typical day is like and how they'll interact with your training courses.

Shadowing Line Staff

To develop accurate personas, combine the information you obtain from HR with what you experience in a typical day on the job with a staff member:

- How often do they have access to computers?
- Do they have previous experience taking online courses?
- When does training typically happen for a staff member?
- Is it practical for the employee to do just-in-time or at point of contact training?
- What are the main issues that staff experience when completing their jobs?

While the last question is beyond the scope of e-learning development alone, it's worth knowing learners' concerns and thinking about how you can mitigate them.

If you have multiple locations, you'll want to visit all of them, but you don't need to spend a whole day shadowing each position at each site. The purpose of visiting each location is to get a sense of the differences in culture and schedule, as well as to ascertain the technological availability.

Should you encounter difficulties getting permission to visit various sites, request to assess the technical situation at each location. You need to review the computers and Internet connection to determine the level and complexity of the content you develop. It will also build a rapport with the line staff, who may not be happy about having to take online training. Humanizing yourself at the outset will create a better working relationship, particularly when you need their help with quality assurance and when they need technical support.

Shadowing the Subject Matter Experts

Subject matter experts have deep knowledge in a particular area of the company and often train other staff on that subject. They can include the payroll administrator (using timesheets), benefits administrator (signing up for benefits), procurement manager (overseeing sourcing and contracts), and risk manager (keeping up with OSHA). Generally, your sponsor—the person who advocated for your position in the organization—will give you an idea of project prioritization, letting you know the people to start with as your SMEs.

Many organizations develop e-learning so that the subject matter experts can provide content to staff without having to do it in real time. That is, the subject matter experts will train you on the content, and you will make it into a module that staff can take when they're interested and available. The subject matter experts will have additional time to work on their regular duties, as well as the ability to spend time on higher-level training, coaching, or individualized solutions.

Spending time with the SMEs will allow you to experience the most common questions they receive, the training they offer most often, and how learners feel about them. Take notes for later discussions with the SMEs to prioritize the training courses that you will develop into e-learning.

If possible, take the SMEs out to lunch, or speak with them outside of work. Find out about their educational background and what makes them the experts. What about the topic inspires them, and how do they stay up-to-date with the latest trends in the industry? Knowing the content sources they use is helpful; you can use them in case you need to add in content during development.

Use your judgment as to whom you have these meetings with. Just because someone is a lead in a particular division or department doesn't mean they have a lot of expertise in that area. I've worked with outside experts when the in-house staff didn't have the information necessary to meet our needs.

The reasons for building a relationship with your subject matter experts are covered in greater depth in chapter 4.

Advice From the Trenches

The first thing I did once my computer was set up and I'd gotten a copy of the organizational chart was to arrange lunch and a meeting with each subject matter expert and several members of the HR and training departments. Usually, I like to have lunch first. I start with a relaxed conversation about my background and some general ideas about training, and specifically e-learning. I find out about them and their organization background, along with their general perceptions of what I'm doing with the organization. A day or two later, I follow up with a formal meeting. Now that we've gotten to know each other socially, it's much easier to start discussing the content that exists and what will and will not be made into e-learning courses and why.

Building a personal connection with staff before diving into the content allows them to trust you and see you as the expert, particularly when you're having more difficult discussions about adult learning principles and why some training programs will need a major change to be effective e-learning courses.

Project Management

If they're available, meet with your organization's project management office to determine the organization's preferred project management style. If that office does not exist, speak with any of the organization's project managers. Should your organization have neither of these, meet with your sponsor to talk about any forms of project management in the organization and how your module development will be best received.

The different styles of project management specific to module development are discussed in depth in chapter 3.

Existing Training

You might be the first e-learning developer hired by your organization, but that doesn't mean you are the first exposure staff have had to online training. And if you're not the first developer, you'll have the opportunity to review the work created or purchased before you started.

When starting at an organization or taking on new e-learning responsibilities, it is useful to do a full review of the current training catalog. This will give you an idea of the level and diversity of content that learners have experienced.

Assess the types of training you find in the catalog and the percentage of overall training available for:

- classroom or face-to-face
- video
- synchronous online (webinar)
- asynchronous online (e-learning).

Once you have the quantities of each of these, do the same thing with attendance records. Speak with management if there is a wide disparity between these numbers. For example, if you find that people almost exclusively attend classroom training, it would be worth investigating the possible reasons. Some of the potential concerns are:

- **Technology availability.** If staff don't have access to computers to watch videos or attend synchronous or asynchronous training, this will need to be addressed for you to be successful.
- **Space.** If there isn't space for classroom courses or for computers to be set up for staff to take training, you'll need to decide how to handle this.
- **Hours.** Are staff members taking more training than has been documented? Maybe they're attending conferences, certification courses, webinars, and so on, but the documentation for this training isn't being recorded in the system of record, or no system

of record exists. This is important information on how staff spend their time and what's lacking in the internal training catalog. It can also help you evaluate the training content and determine return on investment.

Here are a few other topics to consider when evaluating your current training catalog.

Reading Comprehension Level

Many writing programs, including Microsoft Office, will allow you to turn on readability statistics. With this, you can see the Flesch reading ease score and the Flesch-Kincaid grade level. The Flesch reading ease score is a 100-point scale, with 100 being a fifth-grade reading level and 0 being a college-graduate reading level. It is determined by the length of the sentences and the average number of syllables per word in the sentence. Similarly, the Flesch-Kincaid grade level is the U.S. grade level you would need to have reached to read a sentence. While the level theoretically goes to −3.4 (preschool), usually the scores are read as school year and month, so 8.4 would be eighth grade, fourth month.

Having a working knowledge of these scores will be imperative when assessing how prior e-learning materials performed with end users. In addition, with this information, you can adjust any new training programs to ensure they don't score dramatically higher or lower than what the audience expects. Consider including these scores in the personas you develop.

Cultural and Language Localization

Is the current training catalog multilingual? How does your organization handle localization, if at all? If you are not of the same cultural background as the learners, are you comfortable developing culturally appropriate content for them? If not, do you have access to someone who can have a candid conversation with you about what is and is not appropriate?

If your organization provides training only in your native language to people with a cultural background similar to your own, this part is simple. You can develop as you usually would, and it will be appropriate for the audience.

If your organization offers training for a different cultural background than your own, but in a language you're comfortable with, then you can work with someone well versed in that culture to develop appropriate content.

If your organization develops training programs for multiple languages and cultures, find out how they have been localized. Many organizations will have subject matter experts whose backgrounds are reflective of the audience. They may be the resource for localization, or the organization may outsource this work. If that's the case, you need to find out whether you're expected to enter the localized information into the module or if the outside company does that.

When adapting modules for different languages and cultures, note that e-learning developers have a few options. First is translation, which is taking the literal text and changing it to another language. Next is interpretation, or taking the concept of the text and changing it to another language. Finally, there is localization, or changing the concept of the text to make it appropriate for a specific area where the language is spoken. For example, you could translate or interpret a module into Spanish, but with localization, you could be adapting the module for Central Mexico, Argentina, or Southern Spain.

Audio and Sound

Assess the number of modules that have a voice-over. Voice-over is beneficial because it adds another channel, thereby lowering the cognitive load and helping users understand complex information more easily than if they only had access to the visual channel.

Adding audio to the module will increase the development time. It will also require learners to have access to headphones or a quiet space to take the course. More information about audio production is discussed in chapter 9.

Evaluation Types

Next, review whatever method of evaluation your organization uses. Take the evaluation data that you have access to and use that to prioritize rewriting, sunsetting, and developing more advanced training. This will inform the subsequent discussions you have with subject matter experts on the content available and the next steps—either updating or creating more advanced content.

If your organization does not evaluate training, consider how you can add this step to the training programs you develop. For example, the Kirkpatrick model has four generally accepted levels of content evaluation:

- **Level 1: Reaction.** This level assesses how learners rate your trainers and training programs. It provides background information you can use in future development.
- **Level 2: Learning.** This level assesses how well learners acquired the knowledge and skills the training program was meant to impart. If a trainer has a very high Level 1 score, but no one passed the assessment at the end, how effective is the training program? Temper the results from Level 1 with those from Level 2. Also evaluate the assessment the program used—does its level of difficulty reflect the difficulty of the content? If the assessment was simply to ensure attendance, this is something to consider updating in the future.
- **Level 3: Behavior.** This level assesses how well learners apply what they learned on the job. Generally, the goal of training is to change

behavior. Only a small number of organizations assess at this level and above.

- **Level 4: Results.** The most difficult level to gather data on, Results shows whether the training helped create the change that was the initial cause for training.

Information specific to assessment and evaluation is covered in more depth in chapter 12.

Next

The organizational needs assessment only really has to happen once when you first join the organization or move into a training and development role. After you've internalized all the material in this chapter, your next task is to assess organizational and individual employee needs for specific e-learning modules.

CHAPTER 2

Module-Specific Needs Assessment

How does your organization contact you to develop training? In the average organization, particularly for a new employee, there are a lot of requests to develop very specific modules. As you build a relationship within the organization, you'll be able to address and assess gaps as you go. Early in your tenure, start working with the team—which generally comprises subject matter experts, the project sponsor, and interested stakeholders—to help determine the gaps and build the solution to move learners to the desired state.

Each time you develop a new module, a module-specific needs assessment should take place. For several modules developed for the same audience or with the same subject matter experts, you can reuse information from other module assessments; however, this step should not be skipped entirely.

For illustrative purposes, let's say that you are creating a training program for current staff who want to become supervisors. The staff can come from any division in your organization, but have all been at the organization for at least a year. They self-select for the program and are allowed to attend pending their supervisor's recommendation. Beyond that, you determine all aspects of the training and content. This type of training can be developed in any industry at corporate, nonprofit, or government organizations. It can be a program with a number of different modules that are provided in the classroom, through an e-learning course, or a blend of methods.

Determining the Needs

The first step in your needs assessment is to determine why you were asked to create this training program. Ideally, the needs assessment will reveal a gap between learners' current state and the perceived state or behavior that you want them to exhibit.

In the new supervisor training example, the perceived state would be legally compliant and effective supervisors cultivated from the company's internal staff. The gap is that the staff you presently have are unfamiliar with the legal issues and requirements of being a supervisor. The staff members eligible to become supervisors will need to be assessed for the skills to become a supervisor, learn about supervising, and then demonstrate their understanding.

To determine the behavioral outcome of the supervisor training, you would ideally ascertain the validity of the gap with the staff. Shadowing the most effective supervisors and speaking with their supervisors will reveal the exemplary behaviors and habits. It is important to note how you identify effective supervisors. For instance, asking staff members how much they like their supervisor would not be an optimal way to gather this information. You want to focus on the supervisors who perform well on their reviews from their supervisors, and those who build the skills of their staff by allowing them increased responsibility. Interviewing the staff who would like to become supervisors will also help you determine the level of knowledge and skills already present in the organization.

Here's an example: The managers have had four pay cycles, or two full months, to get used to the new payroll system. They have been trained in the classroom, given job aids, and sent emails telling them they have to approve timesheets by 10 a.m. each Tuesday. However, your sponsor notes that fewer than 30 percent of the managers complete the approval on time. Your sponsor suggests you build a microlearning module, "something quick," to resolve this issue.

Is this a good use of your time? You weigh the positives and negatives of the request.

The positives:
- There is a specific issue. It would lend itself well to being resolved with just-in-time training or microlearning.
- There is a behavior that managers need to change. It is observable and measurable, thus allowing for an ROI evaluation.

The negatives:
- The managers might already have the knowledge required to comply with this mandate. Training may not be the correct option.
- Microlearning and just-in-time training would be useful if the issue were that the managers were logging in to approve the time but were unable to do so due to a skill or knowledge gap. If they simply aren't logging in before the deadline, training wouldn't address the issue.

Rather than jumping ahead to develop an e-learning module, you go back to the sponsor and say you don't have enough information to determine that microlearning will resolve the issue.

According to Human Performance Improvement (HPI) expert Dennis Mankin, "Seventeen percent of the time or less is training (of any kind) the primary influence needed to improve workplace performance (based on numerous HPI analysis conducted over at least 20 years); therefore, never lead a performance improvement effort with training unless a performance analysis has been conducted. In other words, 83 percent of the time training just isn't going to improve workplace performance. It may be a minor influence but not the primary influence."

How might the previously mentioned situation have gone differently? Dennis shares his expertise: "Never lead a training analysis and launch an e-learning event based solely on behavior-based or subject matter mentalities and actions. Workplace performance and learning (that is successful in producing measurable results) is based on using results-based approaches and the focus on outcomes of value produced by accomplished or key performers in the workplace."

The first step is to conduct a needs assessment at the module level. Look for the need to be addressed with performance improvement. For this example, it would be prudent to speak to a statistically significant number of supervisors to ascertain if they know when time sheets are due. If they do, then this would become an operational change. If they do not, then you can move into the next steps for determining the appropriate training format.

Working With Subject Matter Experts

Meeting with subject matter experts will reveal specific details about the content, which is what you'll use in the instructional design step to create the training.

Subject matter experts will change based on module content. With a topic like supervisor training, the subject matter experts will likely be a few members from the HR team.

My favorite way to conduct a needs assessment is to get everyone in one room and ask them a series of questions. I have them respond on sticky notes, with one thought per note. Then we put the notes on the wall and group like ideas together (Figure 2-1).

We discuss all the notes with nothing else like them to determine if they are errant thoughts or if someone has realized something the rest of the team didn't think of (Figure 2-2).

Next, we take the notes on a similar theme and rewrite them in a way that everyone agrees on. Given that supervisor training is a complex

Figure 2-1. Sticky Note Needs Assessment, Step 1

subject, this step may take place over the course of weeks or months. The content groupings for supervisor training will encompass areas like appropriate staff boundaries, employee-rights laws, leadership styles, communication styles, and delegation.

Then we build an above the line/below the line analysis on the wall. To do this, put two lines of tape on the wall. One should be about waist level and the other about shoulder level. Everything above the top line is information we either expect learners to know or will include in a training program prior to this one. Everything between the lines will go into the training program in development now. Everything below the bottom line will be put into a future training program learners will complete after this one (Figure 2-3).

Figure 2-2. Sticky Note Needs Assessment, Step 2

Let's apply this line analysis to the supervisor training example:

- Information above the top line could be included in prerequisite courses for less experienced staff.
- Information between the lines could be the main content all staff must demonstrate knowledge of to be a supervisor, and could be included in the training program you're developing now.
- Information below the bottom the line could be optional, extracurricular, or deeper knowledge for staff who would like more information.

Use the information between the lines for the design phase. Give the information from above and below the lines back to the SMEs to determine if it's already addressed in available training or create training requests for future development.

Figure 2-3. Sticky Note Needs Assessment, Step 3

There will be times when it is impractical for you to develop the requested training program. If the audience is only one or two people and you won't need the program again for years, it may be better for a SME to meet with those learners and train them. Maybe the program is not as important as other projects on your list. Or perhaps an external vendor has developed a similar program that meets your organization's needs, and it makes more sense to buy it rather than build it again.

Advice From the Trenches: JD Dillon

Every employee is unique. But as a one-person e-learning department, how can you personalize your training programs to match the different backgrounds, strengths and weaknesses, and learning abilities? It starts with a shift in mindset. You're more than a builder or a presenter—you are a curator, an enabler. Your job is to open and enhance channels that employees can use to solve problems and develop. Yes, you will still build some content, but that's not the way to scale. Rather, you must enable methods that get the right information from the people who know it to the people who need it.

With this mindset, you have several options for how you can balance the push-pull nature of workplace talent development to provide a more personalized experience. First, consider new ways to curate and crowdsource on-demand knowledge. There are people sharing what they know in your organization right now. How can you capture that knowledge and scale it so it becomes accessible to a larger audience? Find those people and figure out how you can make it easier for them to share and help those in need. This will provide employees with the opportunity to personalize their learning and problem-solving experiences, just like they do in the real world using Google and YouTube. Use your curation abilities to find respected, skilled managers and help them share their best practices.

Rather than build or purchase a big content library that no one will ever use, you can focus your time and resources on just the content needed to solve specific business problems as validated by data. Technology can then scale this content so employees get it at the right time based on their development needs.

Learning Constraints and Delivery Method

Now that you have an idea of what the skills gap is and how the experts recommend filling it, what would keep the learners from being successful? Work with the SMEs to determine when and where training can take place. Even though this book is focused on e-learning development, you still should not take the sponsor's word at face value if they want an online training program.

Determine if it's practical for learners to be away from their job for this training course, or if the course needs to happen outside working hours. For the purposes of retention and the scope of training, how much time is practical per session? Does learning everything back-to-back make sense, or should there be time between learning experiences so that learners can reflect on and implement what they've learned?

Discuss these questions with the SMEs and the learners' supervisors. Organize a group discussion to determine what will best meet the content and learner needs. This is also the time to talk about how to share the content with the learners. Traditionally, the options for delivery are classroom training, e-learning, and a combination of the two. Each of these offers tons of options. The initial discussion will give you a basic framework from which you can develop.

When determining whether an employee has learned how to be an effective supervisor, a multiple-choice test probably isn't the optimal assessment. Deciding on an assessment now with the SMEs will inform the instructional design you'll do next. Early decisions of this magnitude will dramatically improve the probability that what you develop now will ultimately meet the organization's needs.

With other design components established, it's time to talk about time. You need to know how soon the organization needs this training program rolled out to learners. Try to be as realistic as possible given the time you'll need for development, testing, approval, and deployment.

If you have chosen to develop e-learning, you'll need to test both the content and the technology.

Approvals and Stakeholders

Now that you have a good idea of the need and the content to address it, you want to make sure you know who approves the final deliverable.

There's nothing better than the feeling of having a project approved and deployed to your learners. And nothing is worse than having a project rejected. When starting out at a new organization, spend time identifying who will approve your content before it goes to the learners. For the supervisor training example, the content lead and the overall approver may be the director of HR. Other C-suite members may also need to approve the training program, depending on the level of supervisory oversight learners would obtain.

The following are the levels of approval you might typically find in an organization:

1. **Initial Content:**
   » **Subject matter experts (will vary by topic).** When you finish storyboarding, have the subject matter experts sign off that the content is complete and accurate.
   » **Content area lead (varies by topic; generally the SME's supervisor).** This person is responsible for ensuring that the content is in line with other training materials.
   » **Final approver (will vary by topic).** Because this module deals with supervising requirements, the director of HR or another HR member will review the content to ensure its accordance with company policies and procedures.

2. **Publication of Module:**
   » **Subject matter experts.** As with the initial content, the subject matter experts should review the module for usability

and content. Because they will likely be the one providing subsequent training, it is important for them to have a working knowledge of the module to address any questions.

» **Quality assurance assistants (employees).** Choose a few tech-savvy employees who work in your office to try out the training material. You can have a few people do this for all the modules or rotate through a group of people.

3. **Publication to LMS:**

» **IT.** IT tests the module on the hardware and in the software that learners will use.

» **Beta testers (end users).** After the SMEs and quality assurance team have approved the module, randomly select a small section of your users. If possible, proctor their training to see what issues they encounter.

Embracing the Reality: Nikki O'Keeffe

When you start an e-learning project, be realistic. You are only one person. Do what you can and rely on others' expertise to fill in the gaps. For example, maybe you outsource the narration, videos, or image creation. As learning professionals, we want to do it all, but it may not be possible with your workload, skill set, or resources.

Next

Knowing the organization, learners, and expectations for training, it's time to start the module development. The first step will be to establish what qualifies as success and ensure that the members of the organization understand the timeline. This is done through effective project management.

CHAPTER 3

Project Management

Each module you create, curriculum you design, and LMS you launch is a project. They all start, proceed as work is done, and end. But is it really important to use a specific project management technique when you're the only member of your department?

Typically, project management helps coordinate teams to ensure that every member knows the activities required to complete an agreed-upon goal. As a department of one, you might think that project management won't add value to your work. However, following a project management framework can clarify projects for you, provide deeper visibility on next steps, better integrate your projects with others in the organization, and help provide metrics for return on investment to management.

Because you're the only resource, your project management style doesn't have to follow a strict structure for development. You may be the only resource as the member of a functional organization, so that each content area has a person doing a similar task to yours, but you don't directly work together (Figure 3-1). Or, you may be the only person in the entire organization who does what you do, and you are developing for all the functional areas (Figure 3-2).

Figure 3-1. Member of a Functional Organization

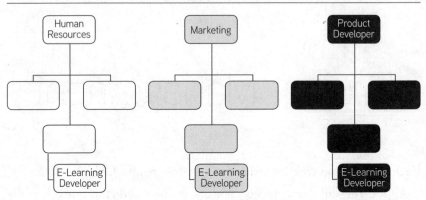

Figure 3-2. Only Developer in the Organization

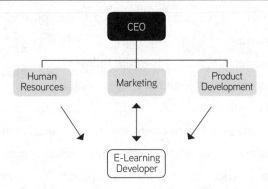

Either way, systematizing the work that you're doing will make it easier for you to know what you're working on and share it with others who need access. The first step will be to figure out how you want this system to operate. Start by writing a list of all the topics for which you are developing e-learning. Then divide each of these topics into categories appropriate to your organization. These might include:

- **Length:** microlearning, intro module, full module
- **Type:** traditional module, interactive video

- **Priority:** due immediately, three to six months out, longer
- **Content category:** human resources, marketing, product development.

Use these categories to help build your prioritization. Most organizations are going to have a person or department whose projects are always highest priority and highest value, at least to them. Having all your projects laid out in a way that allows sponsors to see what you're working on and the estimated timelines will help minimize conflict. As a person who supports the organization in the development of projects, show any sponsors who have conflicts related to their timelines or prioritization exactly what you're working on and allow them to work it out with each other. You are only one person and have only so much knowledge, ability, and time. It can be particularly helpful to start another project while this discussion is happening; it increases the pressure on the sponsors to come up with a solution, because neither of their projects is being addressed.

Effective project management has numerous benefits to your work flow and development. In addition to the clarity it provides on the work that you're doing, it will make it easy for you to transition between projects when you need a mental break. And it will give you an idea of the amount of time that you spend on each project, which will help you assess costs and return on investment.

Research has shown that it takes at least 42 hours to develop an hour of e-learning; a 20-minute course would take 14 hours, and a five-minute course would take 3.5 hours (Defelice 2018). Depending on your level of experience, you can alter these times to your timeframes as you become more familiar with your pace.

Now that you've gotten an idea of what you're going to work on and approximately how long it will take to develop, you'll need to decide how you're going to develop it, which will determine the style of project management that you use.

Styles of Project Management

Let's think about developing a series of modules on new supervisor training. The overall training concept will be to take current staff members and teach them how to supervise staff. At the end of the training program, they will be eligible to apply for supervisory positions. Look at the following two major methodologies for development and consider which you'd choose to create this training program.

When you start learning about instructional design, the classical model that is taught is ADDIE: analyze, design, develop, implement, and evaluate (Figure 3-3). If you have a background in project management, this is roughly the waterfall methodology. You have a defined path that you follow; if something is incorrect in a preceding step, there isn't much you can do about it other than move forward or cancel.

Figure 3-3. ADDIE as Seen Through the Waterfall Methodology

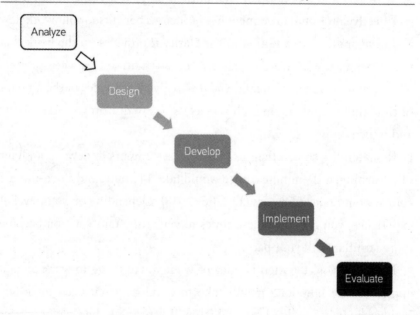

Instructional designers have started to follow the lead of software developers, and some have begun to change their previous waterfall approach to an Agile practice. With a waterfall style of development, particularly with projects that are months in development, by the time a course is available to the learners, the concepts or technology may have changed. Although Agile is more iterative and incremental than ADDIE overall (Figure 3-4), there are two versions of Agile that take a more iterative or incremental approach. You can develop with either the iterative or incremental philosophy, or the two together.

Figure 3-4. Agile Model

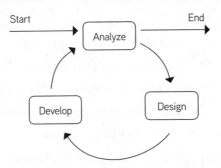

The Successive Approximation Model (SAM), from Allen Interactions, is one iterative development model. It provides a minimum viable product, which the SMEs or learners try out to see how it works. Then a round of development is done to make changes and improve the images and voice-over; the training program is reviewed again, and then given a final review.

Incremental design has the developer divide the content into sections, or modules. The first module is finished, then the second, until all the content is available. A good example of incremental development is creating microlearning on specific topics and then aggregating them into a larger module once they're all completed.

29

As mentioned, the two can be combined, which many developers do. In this case, the construct for the entire concept is created roughly and then developed to completion in sections.

Throughout the rest of this chapter, I use waterfall and ADDIE interchangeably; know that both *ADDIE* and *waterfall* encompass all the options of either style. Let's look at the benefits and drawbacks of ADDIE/waterfall and Agile for e-learning development.

Back to the supervisor training example: How would this work? Let's say that you have cohorts of 30 people and the training will take a year to complete. If you developed this in the waterfall methodology, you'd spend months collecting information about the content. Then you'd design and develop the modules. Once they were completed, you'd beta test them, make changes, and widely disperse them. After the modules were launched, you would run evaluations of the pass rate, knowledge acquisition, and behavior changes to see how effective the content was. Depending on the number of training hours, you're likely looking at around two years of work before content is available to learners.

Creating this same training program in an Agile way, you might develop the modules as the learners are experiencing them. You would still do the initial needs assessment to build the overall structure of the course. You could then adjust the modules as you go. The first group of employees would receive a module, changes would be made based on their feedback, and the second cohort would have an updated module for their first interaction.

Neither one of these methodologies is empirically correct. You could make wonderful and effective training programs with either. An Agile approach can mitigate the drawbacks of having to wait a long time between development and feedback under the waterfall method. On the other hand, an Agile approach can also raise timeline concerns as content gets continuously revised, and subject matter experts can add overwhelming amounts of detail during later revision stages, all issues not present in a waterfall method. It's simply a matter of knowing what works for your organization and the content. Table 3-1 is a summary of the advantages and drawbacks of each method.

Table 3-1. Benefits and Drawbacks of Waterfall and Agile

	Waterfall	Agile
Benefits	• Most widespread approach • Formalized framework • Established process • Entire project is completed at conclusion	• Deliverable is available for review early and often • Customizable to meet the needs of any organization or project • Stylistically similar to software development
Drawbacks	• If the analysis is incomplete, the rest of the project will suffer from incompleteness or inaccuracy, or be canceled • Longer timeframe before a deliverable is available for review	• Optimally need to run three cycles to start project development • Increases the potential for an incomplete or suboptimal final project being submitted to the client

It's important to note that you are not required to stick to one style of project management and use it across all your projects. You'll change the style based on the complexity of the project, the accessibility of your SMEs, and your timelines. Your organization may also have a project management office (PMO) or other organizational process assets (OPAs) that will give you a starting point for choosing a management style for your first few projects. A PMO is the part of the organization that oversees all projects. It can be very useful for finding OPAs.

Advice From the Trenches: Megan Torrance

Agile project management has been around since 2001, if we consider the writing of the Agile Manifesto (www.agilemanifesto.org) as the beginning of Agile in the software development industry. Agile project management is an iterative, incremental process for guiding design and building projects in a highly flexible and interactive manner, focusing on maximizing customer value and fostering high team engagement. The Agile Manifesto set out a framework of values that would enable teams of software programmers to develop software in ways that allowed for changes in underlying needs and a continual discovery of requirements throughout the project effort. If you're working with software developers at your company, it's quite likely that they're using Agile.

With the success of Agile project management in the software industry, it comes as no surprise that learning and development practitioners have sought to adopt it; indeed, LLAMA, SAM, and other project management approaches are less linear than ADDIE. In many respects, the design-build aspect of software design and development is akin to that of instructional design and development, and this holds even stronger when we're developing e-learning or other digital learning experiences. Many teams have implemented Agile approaches with success.

These teams use Agile project management to scope the effort, define the tasks, estimate the work, set a schedule, deliver and release work products frequently and iteratively, and communicate with peers and clients, whether they are internal or external. Thus, it is distinct from the specific instructional design techniques and approaches that you might use, such as Thiagi's 4Door, the Six Disciplines of Breakthrough Learning, Merrill's Principles of Instruction, Allen Interactions' CCAF Model (Context, Challenge, Activity, Feedback), individualized instruction theory, High-Impact Learning, Bloom's Taxonomy, or Carla Torgerson's MILE framework for microlearning. Agile is also independent of the learning modality or medium and can be applied to e-learning, instructor-led training, microlearning, blended learning, performance support, virtual reality, or projects in which we create a social framework for informal learning.

As a cautionary note, there are several key differences between instructional design and software development work processes that should inform your adoption of Agile:
- Instructional designers need to focus on learning objectives and performance outcomes, in addition to functions and features that software developers build.
- Most instructional designers work on several projects at once, while software developers usually are dedicated to a single project.
- Instructional designers often need to wait for content or SME input and have to account for that downtime in their project plans. Agile software teams are typically in a continuous develop-test cycle with little downtime in between iterations.

These differences in the nature of software development and instructional design are sources of frustration for instructional designers in their application of Agile methods, or they lead to the development of new adaptations, such as LLAMA or SAM. Teams that make adaptations in their Agile project management approaches to account for these differences are finding success.

Your Organization's Culture for Project Management

The culture of your organization will play heavily into your development process. If you're at an organization with lots of competing high-priority projects, you'll need to assess the practicality of having three review cycles to effectively implement Agile. If the subject matter experts are difficult to contact and unlikely to give you all the information you need to develop your content, ADDIE might result in inaccurate training. The longer the time from the original needs assessment to the final product, the greater the probability that the information will change.

Here are some questions to help you consider whether ADDIE or Agile is the better project management style. These should be assessed on a project-by-project basis as the priorities and players change.

1. **What is the availability of your subject matter experts for feedback?**
    » **Not much:** Is it not much over a certain period, or are they never available? If you can get a dedicated block of time all at once, you may want to do ADDIE. If it's never much, then you may want to do Agile and fit in your review and information gathering during those short times that they are available.
    » **Lots:** You are very lucky! In this situation, the SMEs are likely going to give lots of feedback and have input on the project, so going with Agile will give them the fastest deliverable and the greatest ability to interact with the content.

2. **How familiar are my subject matter experts with training on this topic?**

    » **Not familiar:** This can happen if the organization is rolling out a new software or new initiative that hasn't been totally determined. In this scenario, you can wait until everything is decided and make this project your only priority to meet the deadline, implementing ADDIE and doing it start to finish in a tight timeline. Or, you could implement Agile knowing that you'll be redoing large portions of the analysis as the product changes and solidifies. If your organization could use the additional support in advocating for the learner's perspective in development, you could offer that with Agile.

    » **Very familiar:** Surprisingly, these tend to be the more difficult SMEs to work with because they're going to get very technical very fast, or they're going to want to cover tons of content that will be hard to incorporate into a single project. You'll want to spend lots of time building the relationship with these SMEs to be able to rein them in without shutting them down. This will be discussed in greater detail in the chapter on subject matter experts. This would be a good case for using an Agile methodology so that you can keep testing different types of content flow and add or remove content as you find gaps or extraneous information.

3. **How experienced are the learners with this topic?**

    » **Novice:** The less experienced the learners are with the content, the more time you'll need to spend in your analysis phase to gauge what they'll need to know before you can get into the content that the SMEs want to cover. You'll probably be teaching terms and acronyms. The beauty of novice learners is that typically the entry-level training will focus on knowledge, which makes the evaluation and assessment easier. You could really go either way with a novice when choosing a methodology. ADDIE might make sense if the audience knows so little that it's easy to come up with the content they'll need. Or, if you're having a hard time assessing the knowledge gaps, Agile would be better to allow for more rounds of user testing prior to launch.

» **Experienced:** Experienced learners will require pretesting to ensure that they have the foundational knowledge the SMEs expect. These training programs typically focus on skills and abilities. The focus of the instruction here is more on scenarios to teach and reinforce what we want learners to do after the completion of the course. Plan to build in lots of time for creating the evaluation and assessment. This would probably work better in Agile because you'll be adapting the content to a variety of learners and experience levels.

4. **Is there a hard deadline for when this content needs to be available?**

» **As soon as possible:** More likely than not, this will be most of your projects. These are the ones that you'll want stakeholders to work with you on to determine actual priority. If you can get all the information up front and have limited edits, ADDIE will be the fastest.

» **On a specific date:** Given the number of projects that you have in the ASAP bin, it'll be important to build in the time that these projects require to maintain the commitments that you agree to upon initiation. These are the optimal projects because you and the requester understand and agree to the parameters of the project. Ideally you'll work with ASAP and "whenever" requesters to get a firm deadline. This will vary between ADDIE and Agile based on the perceived number of edits. If there won't be any, ADDIE works. If there will, Agile is better.

» **When you can get to it:** This is the timeline to avoid at all costs. Work with the requester to get a specific deadline. The people who request these projects are usually the ones who want it as soon as possible but think that they're being nice by not asking for a specific deadline. If you end up in this situation with someone that you can't push to provide a specific deadline, make sure that you're continuously moving on this project even if it isn't with the regularity of the others. This is a situation when Agile feels like the right solution, but you can end up with a bunch of modules 80 percent done that you never finish. Be cognizant of this if you choose to go with Agile, where you get feedback but never find time to incorporate it.

5. **How quickly can I update or revisit the training topic if the content does not meet learners' needs?**

» **Fixed schedule:** When you are supporting many clients for e-learning development, you may find yourself building a long timeline of projects. If you're doing this, it will be harder to build in time for fixes and updates. However, ensure that you allocate time for this or that your final products have a shelf life that's longer than your planning calendar goes into the future. ADDIE works well here because you know exactly what you need to do, can make the change, and publish it.

» **Flexible schedule:** The greater the flexibility in your schedule, the greater the pressure to put out less than optimal projects to keep flow moving forward. Do what you can to avoid this, so you create a product that you're happy with before you launch it to your learners. If you don't have something immediately following your next project, don't waste time or perfect the current project past the point of what you're doing with others. Take this time to focus on your professional development. Agile works well here because you can easily alter the content every time that you look at it.

Make Project Management Work for You

With all the suggestions provided here, it's really about customizing project management to meet your needs and those of your organization. Regardless of what you call it, if it's not adding value, stop doing it.

Planning the Project

The first step in any form of project management is to define the project and acceptance criteria. You need to have a clear understanding of what the sponsor expects you to provide in the end. Do not let them dictate how you go about solving the problem that they have. They should explain the issue to you, and you should be able to determine if it's actually a learning problem, and the best format for resolution. Consider this sample conversation:

SME: We are going to write a module on how to have difficult conversations.
You: What is the goal of the training?
SME: We want supervisors to know how to have a difficult conversation with a staff member.
You: What skills does having a difficult conversation entail?
SME: It will require supervisors to be self-aware. They'd need to be able to identify the specific behavior that they want a staff member to change.

They would then need to articulate that behavior to the staff member in a legal and ethically appropriate manner.

You: Are you saying you need supervisors to identify the behavior in question and have the conversation with their employee regarding that behavior?

SME: Yes, and they have to reflect on how the information is communicated. Some supervisors don't know how they come across, which can become problematic legally. The employee either doesn't realize their behavior is an issue or is offended by how it's presented. Either situation is a problem.

You: Ideally this training will have a supervisor identify behaviors with several employees and get their feedback, right?

SME: That sounds great. It would help if we could coach them if they're doing it incorrectly.

Please note that the length of time and frequency were not mentioned among the questions asked of the SME. As the content comes together and you see the scope of the project, you'll be able to make a recommendation. For this training, you might do a branching project that has a coach to scaffold in content for less experienced supervisors. A simulation might also work well for this project.

In all forms of project management, this first phase is the most critical. Your costs are the lowest and it is the easiest to change all aspects of the project. As a department of one, costs include your salary or time on the task. If you implement Agile, your costs for changes will stay lower than with other forms of project management, but with each iterative cycle, the amount of changes should decrease.

If your projects vary significantly, you'll be determining your project sponsors, stakeholders, communication, and risk plans during this phase. If your projects are within a functional area, this may be something you can set at the beginning of your job that will stay fixed across many of your projects.

Project Sponsors

You probably came to be a department of one because someone in your organization said, "Hey, wouldn't it be great and save lots of money if we hired someone in-house to do all this work that we're outsourcing or that we want developed but can't afford?" This person will be your most important sponsor. They advocated for your position and probably hired you. Ensure that your development aligns with their strategic goals.

The project sponsor will request projects and provide you with their scope. You may have someone who sponsors you as an asset within your organization, or you'll have sponsors like the requester from the SME conversation example. This person will advocate for the things that you need with the executive committee. Spend your time building a strong, positive relationship with this person.

Stakeholders

The acceptance criteria are going to be assessed by the project's stakeholders; it's one of the most important parts of this process. Typically your stakeholders will involve a combination of the following:

- **Project sponsor:** This person reports to the executives on what your "department" is developing.
- **Subject matter expert:** The person responsible for providing the content will need to sign off on the training program's accuracy.
- **Your supervisor:** You'll need to obtain approval from your manager or supervisor for projects you complete.
- **End learner:** This one is easy to overlook when you're new to e-learning development. You need to run the final project in a beta

test with the end learners to ensure that the content is functional and understandable.

- **Technical team:** Having your information technology team involved is particularly crucial with e-learning, and ensures their familiarity with the content for the inevitable support calls they'll receive. As your content becomes increasingly technical, having the team involved early in the process improves the probability of project success.

- **Requester:** In some organizations, you will be booked like another asset of the organization. In this case, the people who request work from you are not your project sponsor or your supervisor.

Communication Plan

Because you are the only member of your department or only assignable resource, you don't need to spend time developing a team assignment or plan. You do need to spend time deciding how and when to convey information to stakeholders.

If possible, share your project information on an intranet, like Share-Point. By allowing the stakeholders to pull information whenever they want without asking you for access, you'll save tons of time answering questions. Unless there is a proprietary reason not to, share all your notes related to the development of your projects in this same space. That way if there's ever a question about why something was done or when a decision was made, it's all in one place. If it isn't feasible to share your notes, consider making folders and shared documents on a project-by-project basis to share information with the stakeholders specific to this project.

If you're implementing Agile, you'll have lots of regular check-ins with stakeholders to show them the latest deliverables and obtain their feedback. With ADDIE, you'll want to schedule something on a regular basis to keep yourself on track.

Risk Management

The biggest risk is, of course, you. If you "go down," the entire project will come to a screeching halt. That said, being the project manager, designer, developer, and all around everything for this project, you're likely to be more cognizant of your availability and needs.

Here's the beginning of a risk checklist you can use as you start each project (Figure 3-5).

Figure 3-5. Sample Risk Checklist

Risk: Me

❑ Vacation Time _____

❑ Family Commitments _____

Risk: Infrastructure

❑ Backup Times _____

❑ System Upgrades _____

❑ Cloud Downtime _____

Risk: SME Availability

❑ Vacation Time _____

Risk: Other Projects

❑ _____

❑ _____

The second biggest risk will be the device on which you work. Unless you're saving to a cloud (and even if you are), you'll want a good backup system. One of the less discussed benefits of working with a team is that it pushes you to save to a network location to allow multiple people to work on or review a file. Unfortunately, with several of the larger e-learning authoring programs, it is recommended to save locally to decrease the probability of file corruption. In a perfect world, your computer would be set to back up regularly to a cloud-based drive. Worst case, you can use backup software to regularly copy files to an external hard drive.

The other risks are mitigated to an extent by the style of project management that you've chosen. If your organization is unlikely to give full information and commit to content at the beginning, choosing Agile will increase your likelihood of a more successful final product than ADDIE.

Asset Management

Asset management is another area where a department of one can get sloppy, and it's important to set up a structure as early as possible. Assets will take up large amounts of hard drive space, and you'll want to ensure access to everything you need without compromising your processing power with limited space.

Ideally you'll store a copy of all the assets together, so a completed project with the editable e-learning authoring files, audio, images, and video will all be in a single location.

E-Learning Authoring Files

Because these are the repository for all the custom coding and games you've created, you'll need to access these frequently to refer to what you've done. Ensure that you save versions in remote locations so that if anything happens to your local system, you still have the editable files.

Audio

The final audio will be embedded within the e-learning authoring file, so keeping the audio for the voice actors separately isn't a requirement long term. Depending on your audience, the audio may be as simple as licensed background music, which could be easily stored on a separate drive or CD and accessed as required. Or it could be as complicated as individual voice actor files that are spliced together in scenes with interactions. This is covered in greater length in the chapter on audio.

Images

As a department of one, having a stock asset library will dramatically improve the quality of what you create, lower production time, and minimize the hard drive space that you'll need to keep available. Unless you're doing major editing to the photos from the library, do not keep them separately. Simply keep a list of the used images and licensing information and delete the files. If you need them again, download them from the library.

If you are creating your own images, consider using external hard drives or cloud storage. Asset management software is particularly helpful for tagging the content for future use. Assuming that you have a limited budget to complete the work, the stock image library and external hard drive are a better use of resources than creating your own images and purchasing a cloud-based asset management system. Of course, this is dependent on your organization and content. If stock content is unavailable, research shows that creating imagery reflective of the audience will be better received than decorative visuals. This is covered in greater length in the chapter on graphics and video.

Video

Video is where you can really get into trouble with space. If you're doing video, you need to plan to have multiple external hard drives. As of publication, Internet speeds do not keep up with real-time video processing, and the corruption rate is too high to be comfortable with editing directly from the cloud. This is covered in greater length in the chapter on graphics and video.

Next

It is not possible to overvalue project management in your position. Don't bury yourself in paperwork, charters, and notifications, but plan to spend a certain portion of each day managing your projects.

As early in the planning of a project as possible, choose the project management methodology that will best serve your development. If it doesn't work, try a different one the next time. Customize project management to work for you, your projects, and your organization.

The members of the organization that will most directly affect your ability to meet your project timelines are the subject matter experts. Building a positive relationship with them and managing (and exceeding!) their expectations will be an important part of your success.

CHAPTER 4

Working With SMEs

If you are your own subject matter expert, then you really are in a small e-learning department! You could find yourself in this situation if you're a classroom trainer who is writing content to share with your class, or in a very small organization that's now making e-learning to save you time. Or, maybe you are an expert in a field and want to share your knowledge with a wider audience, so you bought this book to see if you could do it all on your own! Regardless of how you got here, this chapter can easily help you find a solution. It can be boiled down to one sentence: Be nice to yourself!

It's going to take some time getting used to presenting your content to an audience that you'll never meet and when feedback likely comes after the course is completed. In this case, build a network of e-learning developers who can support you if you have questions or face roadblocks.

But what about when you're not the expert and don't have the SMEs on your team? This is dangerous territory that you might find yourself in when you don't know everything you want to know about a subject but are developing training on it. These training programs will become huge time sucks and should be avoided whenever possible. While you may be a skilled researcher and confident in your ability to find the content you need, you won't have someone with more expertise who can take the training course to ensure that your understanding is accurate and fill in any gaps that you don't realize are there. Hopefully a solid round of beta testing can identify areas for improvement. Your time as a department of one is so precious that you should go this route only if the training program is essential and there is absolutely no way for you to find someone to provide content expertise. This should be a very small percentage of the projects you develop.

For the rest of this chapter, let's assume you're not the SME, but they do exist in some fashion within your team or organization. You might luck into having ones who are always available and interested in the nuances of e-learning and training design. They are fun and inspiring to work with to develop content. They show up to meetings and provide useful feedback. They stay up-to-date on the latest trends and know why they're doing what they're doing. In this case, it's a matter of building a strong working relationship with your expert.

Or, you might get stuck with SMEs who'd rather do anything else besides e-learning. What do you do then?

Inaccessible SMEs

Unreachable SMEs may be out in the field doing research or continuously training on the topic for which you've been asked to develop e-learning. Or maybe they're simply overworked colleagues who haven't been sold on the value of spending time on e-learning development. When the project is a priority, these are the ones you have to chase down to get what you need.

If your SMEs are unavailable because they're training staff—either as a formal, classroom trainer, or informally coaching their own staff or new hires in their division—start by reading the articles and training materials that they provide to the audience now. Attend live training sessions on the topic and ask as many questions as you can. Make notes on the things that you found confusing.

If you can't reach the person at all but need to move forward with the project, you might want to build the storyboard and send it to them for approval. It will give them an idea of how well you understand the concept on which they are training. If the content is wrong, they will want to meet with you to address the misconceptions to ensure the final product is what they want to share with the learners.

You can also backfill with research, but like the situation at the beginning where there was no SME to help you on a particular topic, this should be avoided if possible. At least here you have the person to provide feedback on the content in the review cycle. It is useful to ensure that data tracking is on when you have SMEs like this to know what they did and didn't click on and how they performed taking the final assessment. On more than one occasion, I've received a sign off on a module, but I can tell the SME either didn't complete it or didn't open it at all. In these situations, scheduling meeting time and handing them a computer to take the training while you watch can ensure you get the feedback you need.

In the end, it will come down to prioritization. If the SMEs won't make time to work on the project and you have no way to reach them, then move on. You have other projects that need you and deadlines to meet. Tell the person that without more input, you are tabling the project. Make sure that your sponsor is aware of the change and update project timelines. These are highly unfortunate situations, but they can happen to everyone.

Available but Unsure SMEs

When you have a SME sitting at the next desk who can answer your questions and work through content with you, it's a wonderful experience. The main problem I've run into with this type of SME is them not understanding how long it will take you to code the training into the module. Taking their ideas from a paper-based activity, or even a Power-Point mock-up, to a functional e-learning authoring tool isn't something you can typically do in an afternoon.

Available but unsure SMEs are fun for you because they can be a sounding board for trying out new interactions and different types of activities with the end learners. For example, you and a SME are updating a

PowerPoint module on ethical relationships between supervisors and staff. While the module works just fine—there haven't been sexual harassment or discrimination complaints since it was instituted—you believe that a self-paced module that reads through each line of the policy handbook with a matching game at the end is the most effective way to teach the content. Wouldn't it be interesting to do a module where the learner had the ability to choose their demographic and those of their supervisor and a third-party witness? They could go through a series of interactions in which they can respond the way they think is correct and get feedback from the third-party observer about how appropriate the situation appeared.

As an instructional designer, you know that allowing the learner to "discover" the rules behind the system increases the likelihood of them remembering the content, and that doing it in a scenario-based way will cause the learner to more directly apply the content should they find themselves in that situation. However, SMEs might not have that same background.

This is a great time for you to showcase your knowledge as the andragogy (adult learning) expert. Build the module for the classroom-based version of the training program and ask SMEs to use it in their session. Or, you could facilitate the activity with a small group of employees and have the SMEs watch. You could also ask the SMEs to let you try it in this training program and compare the results from the current class with the new one.

Advice From the Trenches

I love looking at e-learning challenges, other developers' portfolios, and samples of content from authoring tool vendors. It is a great way to see the capacities of the tools I'm using, and it gives me ideas for how I can better provide content to my learners.

When I want to try an activity or interaction that isn't something my SMEs have seen before, I send them the links to what I've found and explain how our content could be used in a similar fashion. Allowing them to get hands-on experience and see how it might work and, more important, what needs to change from the demo version to what our learners will see, dramatically improves their buy-in. It helps me move forward with a new idea.

It's important to help the SMEs believe they can own the interaction or activity so that they can justify it to a learner or speak about it at a conference.

Your Role vs. the SMEs' Roles

When you're working alone, it can be easy for other people at your organization, especially the busy SMEs, to discount the work you do because it seems slower than what is produced by other departments. For example, a salesperson could close a multimillion-dollar sale over the course of a month. A marketing department can build a microsite to address a new industry trend over the course of a week. Share information about your process and the variety of considerations and details required to develop a module with your SMEs to build a strong relationship with them. They'll be clear on what projects are in progress and the status of each. Additionally, be up front about development expectations, from timelines to content to roles (Table 4-1).

Table 4-1. The Differing Roles of the SME and E-Learning Developer

Subject Matter Expert	E-Learning Developer
• How the task is done	• How the content is presented
• Technical jargon	• Explaining jargon
• Acceptable performance levels	• How to evaluate performance levels
• Performance objectives	• Developing course
• Content	• Andragogy

As the content expert, SMEs have the technical vocabulary and knowledge. You are the adult learning expert who can choose the best way to present the content for understanding and application and simplify the jargon into terms and analogies that will resonate with learners. If you have an instructional designer who can fill the role of the adult learning theory expert, you are the technical expert who can create the content online. If you are acting as the instructional designer and the e-learning designer and do not have a background in adult learning, consider studying it to ensure that what you create will be the optimal experience for your audience.

SMEs define what content will ultimately need to be understood, demonstrated, and evaluated. You will build the assessment of that content, as well as the course itself. You can provide different approaches to content that SMEs might not be familiar with, such as simulations or scenarios. Depending on your SMEs, you might want to enlist them to be the "voice" of the module and perform the voice-over work or star in photographs or videos that are used in the module. Asking this at the beginning of the process will help with managing expectations and time constraints.

Advice From the Trenches

I developed an annual training program that I give to new subject matter experts at my organization to introduce them to me, instructional design, and project management. It allows me to build a strong working relationship with them, and helps them understand my goals for our work together. Here's the program's basic outline:

1. Defining our roles: What an instructional design and e-learning developer are and how I can help the SMEs

2. Distinguishing between our roles: What I expect from them and how I will use that information (see Table 4-1 for more information)

3. The instructional design process: Brief overview of ADDIE, SAM, and the Deming Cycle (used by another division in our organization)

4. My questions for development: Defining the value for the learner and the organization (discussed in detail in the next section)

5. Logistics: How to request time on my calendar and where to find my project information

Early on, SMEs need to be aware that the work doesn't stop once you've agreed on the content. First they provide the content. This can take place over the course of a single day or span months of meetings, depending on the complexity. Then you'll develop a storyboard, which the SMEs review. Then preliminary development happens, which involves another review cycle with the SMEs. After that's been approved, you'll beta test the module with learners; this step will likely include another approval cycle for any changes that have to be made. Finally, you and the SMEs will meet after the first month's results are in to talk about how well the training program has deployed and the results to determine next steps.

From an Agile perspective, this meeting would be called a retrospective. You would review the process and what you'd want to do differently in the future. From an ADDIE perspective, the evaluation portion of the process determines the next steps in learning development; you may have to start the ADDIE process again with new content. However you'd like to frame this for yourself, unless you have created completely effective modules using all the SMEs' information, the SMEs will continue to be an integral part of your development. Your sponsor will help you prioritize which modules are developed, so the result of the module evaluation may not lead you to move directly to the next module in the same subject area. However, it will go on your list for future development.

As a department of one, you will be responsible for collecting all required content, developing it into a suitable format for learners, ensuring learners can understand and use the content, and evaluating the module to see if it meets the organization's needs. You won't have time to verify every piece of content your SMEs provide, so you'll want them to cite and provide the necessary background information to ensure that the resulting training is accurate. They'll need to know the latest legislation and how it affects the process or behavior the training is informing. However, you will need to coordinate with HR to ensure that the organization's policies and procedures are reflected in the learning outcomes.

Once you've established the parameters for content and content responsibilities, you'll want the SMEs to agree to review the training as you develop it. If you are not an expert on the training topic, you will be learning the content as you go, so gaps will become apparent during development. Some of them will be easy for you to identify because you won't know how to go from one objective to the next; in that case, you'll solicit additional information from the SMEs. Others won't be obvious to you, but the SMEs should be able to identify them in the revision process. Worst case, you may find some of them in the review cycle.

At the beginning of the project, it's also prudent to review and agree to meeting deadlines. There are few things worse for you than idle time. If you're running several projects concurrently and can't make progress on one due to a lack of information from the SMEs, it could get overlooked for months, leading to potential content changes. Mutually signing off on a project is the optimal way to mitigate this risk.

Now that your SMEs have agreed to the scope of the project and the timeline, you have a number of responsibilities. Solely acting in your capacity as an instructional designer, you'll be developing the learning steps and environment. You'll also be acting as the project manager, keeping the deadlines and budgets for the project.

Sharing your instructional design methodology allows your SMEs to understand your process and will strengthen your relationship. Many will appreciate insight into the work process of other experts. Explain why you're choosing ADDIE or Agile (introduced in chapter 3) and the implications of that project management style.

Advice From the Trenches

When starting a new project, SMEs—particularly if it's their first time working with an instructional designer or helping to develop an e-learning module—are usually excited about the process. I like to start informally by inviting them to tell me a few stories.

Story 1: What happens when the desired behavior or skill isn't known?
I want to hear the reason why we're developing the content we're developing. If it's not something that's known now, why do we need this change? Many times, I receive a

response like, "I think what we're doing now is fine, but government regulations require this change." It's important to know information like this going in, because it means the SMEs may not be invested in the timeline or the content. If what's happening now is good enough, you'll need to spend time gaining their buy-in.

Story 2: Give an example of how knowing or doing this improved a situation.
I'm looking for a case study, whether it's from this organization or another. If this is a brand-new regulation, then try to discuss what caused the change in legislation to make this a new requirement. I use the content from this to build buy-in with the learners (and the SMEs).

Story 3: Give an example of how this is relevant to the learners' jobs.
How often do learners perform this task? What changes will they have to make to their daily work lives to accommodate this change? What is the potential fallout for the learner for being involved in this training? For example, let's think about our supervisor training concept: If a warehouse inventory specialist is selected to join the supervisor training program, how might his co-workers, who have been at the company longer, react? At what point should this employee start acting more like a manager when interacting with his co-workers? Can he still go out for drinks after work with his teammates? While these questions won't necessarily be included directly in the course, they are considerations that need to be addressed in delivery or supplemental conversations with employees.

How to Be a Good Instructional Designer for Your SMEs

It will be useful to understand your SMEs' background in training development. Are your SMEs looking to share content with learners, or do they want them to interact with the content and fundamentally understand and integrate it into their lives and behaviors? I'm not saying the first way is necessarily wrong. That is the way many experts used to deliver content. However, some SMEs are more familiar with the flipped classroom concept or Socratic method of teaching, where the time the instructor spends with the learner is about working through the content and augmenting understanding.

Knowing this will help your working relationship with the SMEs to develop content and make them look and feel good. You both are going to want to create a module that learners like and that meets the objective. Understanding their background will help you ensure the SMEs remain a credible, reliable resource. Beyond that, you have the responsibility for ensuring the consistency of the final product, across different parts of the program.

Here is where you have one of the biggest advantages of being a department of one. Because you are the only content producer, it should be easy for you to ensure that you're using the same terminology, writing style, and progression of content. With e-learning in particular, the navigation will be similar, accessibility will be the same, and compatibility with the end learner's technology will be consistent.

When working with your SMEs, you'll also have the valuable knowledge of the beta testing you've done with the learners on other content modules. Use that to advocate for the types of interactions that have worked well in the past. This isn't to say that you shouldn't try new ideas for development, but you'll be able to identify the issues that may arise and plan for them during your module and content development.

If your SMEs are trainers, attend a presentation they're providing to take notes on the questions they receive, the answers they provide, and the feedback the audience gives. While many SMEs believe the modules they create could be given by anyone and are comprehensive in the content they provide, a surprisingly large amount of information is added when they start talking about the topic and have an audience's energy and questions to contend with. Use these notes in conjunction with the presented content for the development of the final module.

If your SMEs don't train staff directly, you can ask them to teach you the content. It will help them organize their content and think about a logical way to sequence it. The drawback to this is if you don't have the same knowledge base as the target audience, the SMEs may oversimplify the training program for you. They may also not be comfortable training or have experience in this environment and procrastinate due to the stress of this type of project. In that case, another choice is to have a brainstorming session, where you have an in-depth conversation about the content. Even shy or inexperienced SMEs are passionate about their content and generally enjoy sharing their background and stories from it.

Here are three questions that can help guide content development:

1. Will the learner understand this concept?
2. Will the learner find this interesting? (Or, what do we need to do to engage the learner in this topic?)
3. Will the learner need this information?

Advice From the Trenches

Use a story to explain to your SMEs the philosophy of developing content:

Once a learner asked the SME how to ride a bike. The SME responded by explaining how to build a bike. The learner stopped them and asked why. The SME said, "If something should ever happen to me, I want you to be able to build a bike so that you'll always be able to go for a ride for yourself."

Instead of telling you what the new learners should know, have them tell you what actions they should be able to do. In the end, is the goal of the training to have learners be able to ride a bike or build a bike that works?

Use this story to develop a plan around actionable goals or behaviors.

Thinking through these questions and the goal of the training will help in your initial meetings with your SMEs to minimize the number of revision rounds that the course content will need.

Other Connections to Your SMEs

Not all the interactions you have with your SMEs will be specifically about e-learning development. Particularly in smaller organizations, you may find yourself acting as entry-level technical support and be expected to provide guidance and assistance in training-related technology.

Live Online Training

This is most visible with live online training, or webinars. Whether or not your SMEs have experience in this area, live online training is increasing in popularity because it allows learners to ask questions in real time and provides the SMEs with the ability to teach a large, worldwide audience simultaneously. As a department of one, you may find yourself acting as the producer or host for these events, introducing the SMEs and ensuring the presentation goes smoothly. It can also be helpful for you to feed the questions to the SMEs so they don't need to monitor the chat window while providing content to the learners.

For you, there are a number of benefits:

- You experience the SMEs' content firsthand.
- You build a strong relationship with the SMEs by making them look good to the audience.
- You experience learner questions, so you know where the gaps are in the current presentation for when you adapt it to e-learning.
- You experience learner commentary, so you know who might be good for beta testing future content, contacting for cases, and using as learner personas.
- You can test quiz and polling questions.

If your SMEs haven't provided training in this format before, you can use your expertise to help them work through their content and allow for regular interactivity with remote learners. Depending on the size of the audience, you could facilitate breakout sessions where learners can work on individual activities and come back and report to the larger group.

Multimedia Development

You have a lot of great skills that can be helpful to other parts of the organization. Because of the tools and technology you use, you may find yourself developing anything from headshots for the website to marketing videos to how-to videos for your organization.

If your SMEs do conduct presentations, you may find yourself building graphics, animation, or the entire presentation for their classroom-based training. I've even offered to redo their presentations to improve the graphics with the stock art libraries I have access to or what I can create. They may also appreciate you adding interactions into the presentations that they hadn't considered, like recording the screen to show how to do something and inserting it into the PowerPoint presentation so they don't have to drive and talk simultaneously.

Next

Your job centers on the development of e-learning modules. Developing e-learning is a small facet of training, which is probably less than 25 percent of what your SMEs need to do on a weekly basis. While moving the project forward will feel critical to you, it is unlikely that your SMEs will prioritize the project nearly as much as you would like.

Maintaining open, regular communication and immediately addressing concerns will build the trusting relationship that will allow you many successful projects with your SMEs. They are invaluable to the content development process—your next step—so do what you can to cultivate your relationship.

CHAPTER 5

Content Development

Now you know about your organization and your potential "customers," the content that needs to be communicated, the people who can provide expert guidance, and how you can run the project to get it there. It's time to start the meat of the work on the project: preparing to design and develop the content.

According to the ATD Competency Model, instructional design is designing and developing informal and formal learning solutions using a variety of methods (ATD 2014). Proper instructional design means being able to:

- Conduct a needs assessment.
- Identify an appropriate learning approach.
- Apply learning theory.
- Collaborate with others.
- Design a curriculum, program, or learning solution.
- Design instructional material.
- Analyze and select technologies.
- Integrate technology options.
- Develop instructional materials.
- Evaluate learning design.

Chapter 2 covered the needs assessment portion. This chapter will go through the rest of the process and see how it can be done effectively in a limited-resources environment. (Chapter 8 will cover technology options more thoroughly, while chapter 13 will describe your assessment and evaluation options.)

Identify an Appropriate Learning Approach

A lot of the data you'll need to identify the appropriate learning approach will come from what you collected during your needs assessment, as well as your chosen project management philosophy. Determine the instructional design model that will best bring these components together, taking into consideration the stakeholders for the module being created, the project management style of the organization, and the availability of the content, both in terms of existing training and the availability of the subject matter experts.

Consider the implications of creating or changing the current training program to e-learning, including the effects on learners. There may be needs that fall outside an e-learning developer role that will nevertheless have to be considered for the success of the implementation, such as the support of a change management philosophy.

Apply Learning Theory

Simply put, learning theory is the way that people learn. There are nearly as many theories about how people learn and the best way to teach them as there are PhDs in adult education and instructional science.

No one theory is likely to dominate all the development that you do. Depending on the complexity of the content and the sophistication of the learner, a combination of theories is useful in your development portfolio. Here are several to get you started, but there are literally hundreds of books on learning theories and the value of each. If you're interested in the psychological underpinnings of learning and how to optimize it, you won't run out of things to read. What's important to remember is that when moving learning content online—whether it's a webinar, an asynchronous course in an LMS, or a video series—you still need to adhere to the proper learning theories.

Andragogy (Malcolm Knowles)

Andragogy is to adults what pedagogy is to children. With an adult, it is assumed that you have some life experience, which you'll use when learning a new concept to build a stronger mental connection to it and be able to use it. Using andragogy in the new supervisor training example, we might ask learners to think about a time they had a disagreement with a family member they respect. Thinking about difficult conversations and the need to maintain the relationship with the family member, how were they able to resolve the conflict? Now taking that same idea, how would that work if you are having a disagreement with a subordinate at the office? Can the same tactics be used? Why or why not?

You're drawing on the learners' life experience. Whether the solution they provided would be useful at work, they are making connections to things that would be appropriate or not in the workplace and understanding why.

Experiential Learning (David Kolb)

The idea behind experiential learning is that learners should literally experience the content to be able to internalize it. With virtual reality (VR) and augmented reality (AR) becoming prominent in the e-learning space, this theory is increasingly practical.

Consider this immersive scenario: Let's say you have an employee who is continuously tardy, and it's adversely affecting the team morale. You put on a set of VR goggles and find yourself sitting at a desk; a woman walks in and starts telling you she's having transportation problems that make it difficult for her to start on time. You, as the learner, have to tell her that this behavior is affecting others and it needs to change. It's realistic and uncomfortable, but allows you to really see what the situation would be like.

As the e-learning developer, you could even take this a step further and record learners' responses. The learner could then meet with a coach to discuss how they might have handled the situation better.

Flipped Classroom (Alison King)

A flipped classroom would be used in a blended learning environment. The idea behind this is that learners do the "homework," or study and practice the content, before attending the session with the expert. Instead of the expert spending classroom (physical or virtual) time explaining the concept to learners, they answer questions and facilitate practice activities.

Consider using the flipped classroom for teaching terms or learning the rules for a new supervisor. Adults being considered for a supervisory position don't need the director of HR reading them pages from the employee handbook. Their time could be better spent going through cases and the implications of each for the individuals involved and the organization.

Model of Hierarchical Complexity (Michael Commons)

With the model of hierarchical complexity, learners start with a very basic concept that is explained in increasing depth and complexity as each task is passed. The theory is similar to the way you'd teach way a child to read, by starting with letters, then phonics, then words.

Teaching new supervisors how to use the time and attendance system with this theory might look like this:

1. Learners can clock in and out as themselves on the timeclock.
2. Learners can clock in and out as themselves on the computer.
3. Learners can approve their own time on the computer.
4. Learners can request time off.
5. Learners can see their employees.
6. Learners can approve their employees' time off.

7. Learners can approve their employees' time for the week.

8. Learners can alter employee time to reflect time worked.

9. Learners can review, alter, and approve time of employees two steps below them.

10. Learners can review and approve payroll cycle for all subordinates.

Systems Thinking (Ludwig von Bertalanffy)

Systems thinking is a big data way of processing information that doesn't add up the parts to make the whole, but looks at the whole completely.

For supervisor training, this might involve showing learners how the various departments in the organization relate to one another and the interactions that cause the organization to be successful or not. The goal would be to show learners that it isn't about removing divisions, but about optimizing the entire organization to make it stronger.

Transformative Learning (Jack Mezirow)

With this theory of transformative learning, learners are placed in a situation that causes them to experience an aha moment upon its conclusion. It's a more pleasant and effective way of changing their mindset about a situation, rather than telling them they're wrong.

As new supervisors, learners might think that it would be appropriate to maintain friendships with their staff members who had previously been their peers. Let's say that a new supervisor, Mary, and her new subordinate, Brian, go out to lunch once a week to catch up on life and talk about their families and situations. When raises are announced and Brian gets more money than another subordinate, John, there is the perception of impropriety regardless of the real reason why Brian may have earned more.

If you follow the theory, you would tell the story to learners from John's perspective. When they hear that Brian got more money than John did, they'll be able to see why that might be a perceived problem and why the organization does not want supervisors and their employees to fraternize.

Collaborate With Others

This is the point when you and the subject matter experts meet to discuss the content. Before getting too deep into the learning objectives and goals, the first step is to identify the content that everyone thinks will be included. Take the sticky notes from the needs assessment in chapter 2 and work through the information "between the lines" to see if you have information that makes sense together and address any of the gaps. Then continue this conversation into developing the story-board (in chapter 6) and designing the program.

Design a Curriculum, Program, or Learning Solution

To design an e-learning solution, you first need to set the learning objective. A learning objective describes the value a course holds for learners. Even for the most minimalistic microlearning, there is some learning value to taking the course, or it would just be entertainment. The objectives don't have to be formal for every course created, but with more complex and detailed topics, providing them allows learners to see what they're expected to know and how they'll be assessed on the learning material.

For example, the supervisor training program will cover a broad scope of knowledge and skills and take place over the course of months. You wouldn't expect to learn everything about becoming a supervisor in a two-hour course. More important, no one wants a supervisor whose only experience is a two-hour course.

In one case, a learning objective might be that by the end of the new supervisor training, the learner (supervisor trainee) will be able to identify and implement the appropriate communication style when speaking to an employee in a disciplinary setting. The enabling factors behind this learning objective include:

- knowledge of communication styles
- knowledge of the employee's personality
- identification of a situation as disciplinary
- identification of the communication style that best addresses the employee and circumstances for the disciplinary meeting.

Keep in mind as you are working through the content what the learner wants to know: Why am I taking this course? What am I supposed to do with this information? How do I prove that I know it? These questions should factor into how you develop the learning objective and how you decide to measure the training program's success or failure.

These questions are usually presented as What's in It for Me?, or WIIFM. The objective could be explained to learners as "knowing how to run disciplinary meetings with the least likelihood of emotional outbursts from employees." This is a very clear benefit to anyone who has witnessed the aftermath of an unsuccessful disciplinary meeting. Because it's a role where they could potentially be the targets of this emotion, you'll have current supervisors signing up in addition to the new ones.

Advice From the Trenches: JD Dillon

Pushing one-size-fits-all training is not enough—even for an L&D team of one. Giving something to everyone just to say that everyone got something does not provide value. By evolving your mindset and expanding your toolkit, you can provide a more personal, right-fit experience for every employee.

One of the fundamentals of adult learning is giving learners the right to choose what and how they learn. There are platforms that will help provide the content you develop in a way to set learners up for success based on their previous choices. When you find yourself in a situation where everyone needs to take the same training program because of a particular requirement, you can still customize the experience with a variety of options. It's a matter of scaling the workload based on the number of people who could follow any particular choice. You don't want to find yourself developing content that only one or two people will want to read, because it's not a good investment of your time.

Analyze and Select Technology

In the needs assessment, you should have determined how and when the learners will access the content. The way you develop content will be different for each platform, whether it's a mobile, just-in-time, on-the-job module or a scheduled training course learners take at their computers. Again, the type of content should be determined before this step.

You might develop a module on difficult conversations for supervisors that outlines *how* to have a conversation with an employee on various unacceptable behaviors or unmet expectations. The complexity and nature of this training program may cause SMEs to suggest that it be a singular module, ideally taken in one sitting on a computer.

Supplemental materials remind and support supervisors when they need to have a specific conversation with an employee. This could be a short training course taken on their mobile phones right before having the conversation with the employee. This module may also not need to have sound; that would require learners to have headphones so other people don't hear the content while they review it.

At this time, you'll also want to establish the types of phones, computers, and browsers learners use to take the modules, how you will be able to do quality assurance testing and on which devices, and how and who will provide technical support for users who don't have access to those devices.

Develop Instructional Materials

With the objectives and technology established, the next step is to choose which e-learning format will best fit your content, organization, and timeline. The traditional types of e-learning include:

- **Websites.** This is the real beginning of e-learning; the ability to share knowledge digitally started with traditional websites. E-learning is still available through websites, but also in SharePoint and web apps, to name just a few other options.

- **E-learning authoring tool module.** In 2002, screen-capturing software evolved into e-learning authoring tools. Developed to allow for interactions with content, this type of training is what people typically think of when talking about e-learning. New versions of this software allow for development simultaneously for computer, tablet, and mobile device.

- **Games.** Traditional e-learning developers have added games or game-based components, called gamification, in two different ways. The first is having learners earn points and compete with one another using scoreboards and leaderboards. Leveling through the content as they learn more and more, the learners are excited to continue and motivated to win. The second way, which can be combined with the first or entirely separate, is adding a game aspect to the content, such as reviewing information with a *Jeopardy!*-style interaction, or moving along a path, like in Candyland. The most recent foray into gamification is the development of full worlds where the content and story are completely connected, like you would see on gaming platforms.

- **Livestreamed content.** If it's important for SMEs to train a large number of learners at the same time, particularly for something with very little turnaround time, livestream can help you do that.

It also has the benefit of allowing a distributed set of learners to ask questions together, and everyone can receive the answers simultaneously.

- **Augmented and virtual reality.** When an immersive experience will enhance the content, AR and VR are the closest you can get to having the learner actually experience the situation in real life. These are the most expensive to build and deploy due to the newness of the development tools and equipment. As mobile phone technology continues to develop, mobile phones in cardboard goggles will continue to make this more accessible and affordable.

Determining the Appropriate Length

You'll determine the training length using logical breaks in the content as you complete development. There are parameters to consider, such as time regulations and how and when learners will take the course.

SMEs should not dictate length except in the broadest of terms; for instance, saying that the content can be learned in two two-hour modules would not be appropriate. You should be skeptical when SMEs or other stakeholders become overly focused on the length without regard to the content. They may guide you toward developing longer courses or microlearning based on the audience and content, but this is a decision you make together as you develop the course, not in advance.

Time Regulations

Many government organizations have time minimums for what they deem to be an appropriate length for adult learning. Just because you have to have a minimum of an hour or several doesn't mean that learners have to complete it in a single sitting. Training can comprise multiple components that add up to the time requirement.

How Learners Will Take the Course

If learners are taking the course on a mobile phone either right before or while completing a task, they won't want a long lead-in about learning objectives and goals. In fact, even an assessment is unnecessary because they are performing the skill while they do the training. The course should be the length of the task or the minimum amount of time to offer the knowledge necessary to perform the task.

When Learners Will Take the Course

If learners block off time to take the course, it can be a different length and serve a different purpose than if they fit it into their schedule. Bear in mind learners' situations and how long they have. If you are developing on-the-clock training for retail employees, every minute they're off the floor is a minute a customer might not be served. Develop for your audience and their needs. Take the time that the content needs and no more.

Learning Styles

Kinesthetic, auditory, visual, reading/writing: You've heard of the various learning styles that individuals may prefer when learning content. Recent research has shown that this is not the case. There is an optimal method for acquisition of content, and that's how people learn best.

Think about learning a martial arts move. For an auditory style, the teacher explains the move while they demonstrate it. For visual, they show the move several times at different speeds so learners can walk around and observe it. For kinesthetic, learners try the move themselves over and over until they become comfortable with it.

Does that mean that the reading/writing learners won't understand the move? Of course not.

What if you were given a book that explained the move? Would you be able to demonstrate it after you'd read about it if you're a reading/writing learner? Of course not.

No one channel is optimal for all content. It's the content that dictates the optimal ways for a learner to process it. Generally speaking, using multiple channels allows for deeper understanding and connection, which is what learners need.

For e-learning, this means that the best way to teach something isn't going to be writing all the words on the screen (visual) and having a voice-over (auditory); aside from being incredibly boring, it won't meet the needs of all learners. You'll need to consider any audio content's accessibility (see chapter 11) to ensure that it meets the needs of any learners with auditory impairments. Beyond that, like with a good classroom presentation, the screen should have, at most, minimal written bullets to augment the talking.

Look back in the chapter at the discussion of learning theories. The learning theory that you've chosen to present this particular piece of content will inform the way to share the information with learners and use as many channels as are practical and useful for the content.

To reinforce the content with learners, consider adding reflective areas where they can take notes, either within the module itself or separately, on how what they've learned will affect their future practices, and what they will change and by when to use this new content.

Sequencing Content

In the needs assessment chapter, SMEs gave you sticky notes and grouped them into like content areas. Now you need to determine the best way to provide those content areas to learners.

Start by asking the SMEs how they think the sticky notes should be ordered. Ask lots of questions and see if there are gaps in the logic or understanding. Make suggestions about rearranging the content.

Once you've got a sequence that seems to make sense, gather several potential learners. Ask the SMEs to sit in the back of the room and walk the learners through the content. See if they're able to understand and demonstrate the desired result from the training course. If they are not, work with the SMEs to address their questions. When they've left, build the additional content and run the test again. Continue this cycle until the learners are able to follow the thread of the content without the SMEs' support.

To give your learners the best chance of remembering and applying the content, you need to build an emotional and job-specific connection.

Emotional Connections to Content

Stories are a wonderful way to draw in learners, particularly with less engaging content. Consider the following two examples for a new supervisor on what to do when an employee says their workload is too high.

Traditional Training:

- **Document.** Keep notes on when complaints are made and the work in progress.
- **Listen.** What are the specific complaints? Don't make suggestions. Gather information first.
- **Investigate.** Are there changes in the employee's workload? Work with the employee to resolve it.

Story Training:

You are a new supervisor of a department of six people. One day, you hear Donna, a team member, complaining to another team member about how she is completely overworked and has too much to do.

The workload seems fairly flat to you. You've been getting to know the team and haven't materially added to what each person does. You've started meeting with the team members, but you don't know them very well yet.

How do you respond?

- Ask her to join you in your office to discuss her feelings right now.
- Ignore her. She complains about everything.
- Keep your regularly scheduled meetings with each member of the department and bring it up then.
- Start a conversation with the team together right then to see if they all feel this way.

In the story version, you can identify with people with whom you work. The interaction allows you to think about what you might have experienced as an employee in a similar situation and put yourself in the shoes of the supervisor and what you think would be the best response.

In either training option, learners can gather the same information. The traditional option gives the information in a completely push manner. Learners can either listen and read along or not and the training progresses.

In the story-training option, learners are unable to progress until they make a decision. The decision will provide feedback and potentially expand from there down a right or wrong path, ending with feedback. The game-like atmosphere will allow learners to safely experience a stressful situation and figure out how they might have done better, or why a particular option isn't the best.

You can use either of these options as the basis for training, and make them more engaging through the activities you develop.

Next

With the groundwork laid for how to develop the content for your e-learning program, it's time to turn to how you might storyboard the content to best convey its message. This involves developing personas and writing scripts.

CHAPTER 6

Storyboarding

Up to this point, you have met with experts and gathered the content learners need to know. You have narrowed the content down to the topic that will be covered in this module. With a storyboard, you're organizing the content and adding the narrative and visual design. This is where your expertise plays a critical role. It's the difference between deciding to create a PowerPoint presentation with voice-over or an interactive experience. Either of these can convey content to the learner, and depending on the learner and the content, might be the right decision.

Storyboarding is the step where you test your ideas for design and style with the SMEs. As a department of one, what you do with storyboarding really boils down to the complexity of the content, the level of access you have to your SMEs, and your working relationship with them. The highest level of access and clear communication between you and your SMEs allows you to start development sooner and spend less time on the storyboard.

If you and your SMEs know one another well and you can communicate functionality that's new to them in a way they understand, storyboarding can be a smooth validation phase. However, every person and content type will be different. Just because you can use a simpler storyboarding interface for one project doesn't mean you'll want to do the same thing on the next project, even with the same SME.

Regardless of the project management approach you take to content development, a storyboard is critical. What would you do if you learned a fancy new software or skill and immediately started developing the instructional content, only to find out that your vision doesn't work logistically? You've wasted hours of time working on something that could have been figured out far more quickly had you laid it out on paper—storyboarding—before moving into development.

If during storyboarding you determine that your hourlong module has six activities and you need to buy 25 stock photos, you'll have a pretty good idea going into development of how long the project will take. If you start off developing and don't have a very clear picture of where you're going, the project could drag on and on. Think of all the time that you spend in this phase as saving you time fivefold in actual module development. It's far easier to change words on a screen or in a PowerPoint file than it is to reorganize a Captivate file or change the clothing on a character in an animation down the line.

Storyboarding will also help you define the different content paths that learners may take based on their individual interests and knowledge. Think about the new supervisor training example. This is a huge topic that encompasses a lot of information and should be different for each person taking it depending on their industry experience, department, and personality type. Imagine two learners sitting at a computer taking this course. What would you make different to address their specific knowledge gaps? Content customization will keep learners engaged and improve their retention.

Finally, without a storyboard, you may leave out sections of content, or have branching scenarios that don't connect back to the main line of content. The storyboard gives you the opportunity to think through everything you want to cover and everything learners may want to do.

When to Storyboard

Depending on the content, you may not need to build a storyboard. Let's review questions that'll help you decide whether one might improve your design (Figure 6-1).

Figure 6-1. Do You Need a Storyboard?

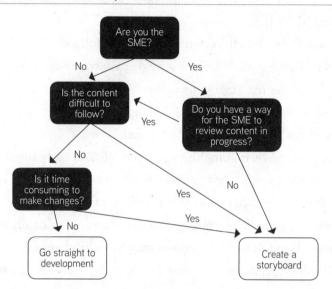

Decision Point 1: Are you the SME?

- **Yes:** If you know the content and learners and are familiar with andragogy, you can decide what content needs to be covered, when, and how, which could lessen your need to storyboard.
- **No:** If you don't know the content, it will be harder to identify gaps in content and logic without a storyboard. You may potentially waste time developing an incomplete or, worse, unusable module.

Decision 2: Do you have a way for the SME to review content in progress?

- **No:** Without a way to easily share content with SMEs, it will be hard to get their feedback, meaning it would be simpler for you to provide a storyboard for approval.
- **Yes:** If you're the SME, you would of course be available to review content. But it's also great if your SME is someone else who's available. Either way, while this doesn't rule out a storyboard, it's a step in the right direction."

Decision Point 3: Is the content difficult to follow?

- **No:** If your module follows a single path where every learner experiences the exact same content, it will be easier for you to review the module directly (although hopefully not many of your modules will have this limited scope).
- **Yes:** If a SME is going through a module and finds an error, the time on task won't necessarily tell you where they are in the module so you can make changes. Slide numbers or some other way to define the navigation would be helpful in this situation.

Decision Point 4: Is it time consuming to make changes?

- **No:** If changes are quick and easy to make, then you can go straight to development without building a storyboard.
- **Yes:** The longer it takes to make changes, the more you may need a storyboard. Do you want to spend lots of time writing JavaScript to make content work the way you want it to, only to find that the SMEs want the information rearranged?

That said, I storyboard all training that's more than 30 minutes long. For microlearning, it depends on my understanding of the content and how difficult it is to make changes to the final product.

Developing Personas

It's useful to start the storyboarding process by developing personas. If you don't know your staff well or it's a particularly large organization, go to the HR department and find out the demographic and psychographic information they keep on file for staff (this process was discussed in chapters 1 and 2). Next, work with the SMEs to identify the data you'll need to build the course. Ask the SMEs:

- Which staff members are expected to take this training?
- Which languages need to be offered?
- How do you expect them to take the training? (what device, paid or unpaid?)
- What background knowledge is expected prior to attending this training?
- Is this training required? If so, can staff members test out? What is the timeline for the requirement? (within a certain number of days of something happening?)
- What state, local, or organizational policies or requirements affect this training?
- How will we assess if the training is successful for the individual?
- How will we assess if the training is successful for the organization?

Make as many personas as you need to reflect the audience that will take the course. Build personas that are fully formed characters. Reading a persona should allow someone else to picture the person when they read it.

Give the person a background. For instance, describe their education, work history, languages, age, and technology experience. What is their current job? What are their career goals? Finally, give them a name. It can also be useful to include a picture of a stock character to represent them. Repeat this process for each audience type.

Figure 6-2 offers two examples of audience personas.

While you develop the storyboard, think about how each person would go through the content and where they would get stuck or need more information.

Figure 6-2. Sample Personas

Seth Jennings

Sales Assistant
Omaha, NE office
Four years with company

Demographics:
- Native English speaker
- Caucasian
- 31 years old
- $32,549
- Omaha, NE
- BA in journalism
- Married six years

- Goal: Run central sales division in five years
- Fear: His co-workers won't see him as a manager

Sarah Gonzales

Customer Service Specialist
Austin, TX office
Two years with company

Demographics:
- Native Spanish speaker
- Latina
- 23 years old
- $24,805
- Austin, TX
- AA in computer science
- Single

- Goal: Customer service lead this year, manager in two years
- Fear: Concerned about her education and language skills holding her back

Images courtesy of eLearning Brothers

Storyboards in Practice

At a minimum, the storyboard will generally show the onscreen content, learner interactions, and the voice-over. Depending on the type of training you're making, you may have content sections followed by activities to reinforce it. In that case, you can call out the general activity and its goal, without specifying details. After the storyboard is approved, then you can plan, develop, and get approval for the activities.

The level of detail in my storyboards varies based on my final output, but I usually start with a simple text file that includes a table with a few headers, such as the slide number, onscreen visuals, interactions, and voice-over text.

When working with more complex graphics, I use a PowerPoint file. The beauty of working in PowerPoint is that it is easy to rearrange slides as I work (Figure 6-3).

Figure 6-3. Sample Storyboard Page in PowerPoint

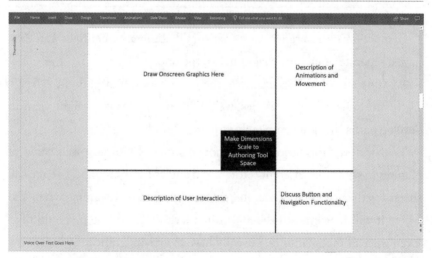

When I'm developing a branching scenario, the storyboard can become complex. Typically, I develop the through-path (all the slides everyone has to view) with slide numbers, and then I use letters to represent different path options. For example, in a scenario that requires learners to return to the main path to answer questions, my Word file might look like the sample in Figure 6-4.

Figure 6-4. Sample Storyboard With Branching Scenarios

Slide Number	Onscreen Visuals	Interactions	Voice-Over Text
22	Choose the best option A B C		
22A	This is the best answer!		
22B	This is an OK answer, but there is a better one.		
22C	This is not a good answer. Try again.		
23	Now this happens next.		

In more-involved branching scenarios, I'll number sequentially and then have a separate branching diagram, like the one in Figure 6-5.

As you can see in this example, there's only one best path: 1, 2, 5, 13. In the next chapter, on activities, we'll look at how far you might want to develop paths that are completely wrong.

With video, it can become even more complex. I typically use a series of pictures to show the different settings and angles I want to tape. I create call sheets for the actors (staff members) to know what we're taping, when and where it will happen, and the approximate amount of time it should take. Even with all that planning, I usually have to arrive significantly before the actors for setup and stay much later for teardown. And editing generally takes five times as long as the recording time.

Figure 6-5. Sample Complex Branching Scenario

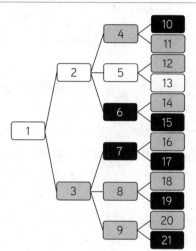

Writing the Storyboard Script

With the content organized, you can now use your expertise to develop the training program itself. Taking the logical divisions in content and separating them into unique modules, you can write the storyboard and script for each module.

When writing a script, there are a number of best practices to keep in mind:

- Use action verbs, present tense, and active voice:
  - » Boring: The child's hands were washed.
  - » Better: The child washed his hands.
  - » Best: Julio washes his hands for 30 seconds, scrubbing under his nails.
- Use a language level that is appropriate for your audience. If you use the Flesch reading ease score, you'll want to aim for at least 60; most popular text is 60 or higher. (News is in the 50s.) If you use the Flesch-Kincaid grade level (year and month), you'll want to aim for around ninth grade. This chapter is 8.3, for example.

- Paint a picture with your words. Help your learner emotionally connect:
  - » Boring: Lifting with your knees decreases the probability of damaging your back.
  - » Better: When picking up a box, squat, pick up the box, and stand up.
  - » Best: Have you hurt your back by lifting something too heavy? Avoid that pain by lifting heavy loads correctly. The goal is to keep your back straight and lift with your hips. Picture your body as a triangle. Your hands and feet are two points of the triangle, with your hips as the top. Squat down, pick up the load, and stand up. No pain, all gain!
- If you're writing the script for a voice-over, try reading the content out loud. When you're writing for speaking, the text may seem fine in your head, but sound strange when you hear it.

If you're not comfortable reading aloud to yourself over and over, or if you're in an office where that isn't an option, Microsoft Office has a feature where it will read the text to you in a variety of voices.

Testing the Storyboard

The most effective way to test the storyboard with the SMEs is to read it to them. Walk them through the onscreen visuals while reading the voice-over. Have them all attend the same session to review the content, and do not send it to them ahead of time. You want all their first impressions together so they can discuss the content in real time and determine if it meets the need. If they get off track, use the training goal from your initial meeting to ensure they are limiting their scope to this specific module.

If you have not had regular access to your SMEs while you're designing the training program, this is where you'll identify the logical errors or misunderstandings you have from your initial communication. It is imperative to do this step because you do not want to spend time developing content that is ultimately unclear, incomplete, or downright wrong.

This is usually the time when the SMEs first think through the content in sequence with you. If you are a member of the target audience, this is a great time for you to ask questions as you're reviewing the content to find out if what you're asking is something that needs to be directly addressed, can be added in as optional information, or isn't relevant to what the SMEs need to communicate.

Make changes as you go so everyone has heard what will be the first-round review content by the end of the meeting. Then, if time permits, run through the entire storyboard again with the team and see how they feel about the changes. If the changes are dramatic and you need time to rethink the interactions, plan another review meeting before beginning the development stage.

Tools for Storyboarding

Start with the paper sticky notes until you are comfortable with the content arrangement. From there, you can move to a digital platform I've described in this chapter, such as Microsoft Word or PowerPoint. Other companies have developed software that is specifically for e-learning storyboarding development, particularly branching scenarios.

Next

Storyboarding can be quite fun. It's when you take every piece of information that you've gathered from the SMEs and lay them out until they make sense and have a cohesive storyline.

Once you have a storyboard and script for your e-learning product, it's time to consider how you can supplement the instructional content with activities to engage your learners.

CHAPTER 7

Building Activities

A good e-learning course will have activities, because they're an opportunity for learners to demonstrate their understanding of the learning objective. Depending on the type of course you're developing, you can use such activity options as branching scenarios, simulations, interactions, and games.

Picture this: You must effectively communicate to an employee that they are not meeting your expectations for timeliness and that their behavior needs to change, or you'll have to take disciplinary action. While experienced managers might know how to have this conversation, for a first-time supervisor, this can be a terrifying prospect, particularly if they now supervise the people that were once peers and that they still consider friends.

What are the best instructional design modalities and techniques to convey the proper way to have performance conversations? A new supervisor is unlikely to succeed if they just listen to a sample conversation and then emulate it at work. A better approach would be to offer a series of activities to complete.

Branching Scenarios

In a branching scenario, an employee comes to the learners with a problem. Learners must respond to the employee from a series of onscreen choices that have both organizational and employee-relations implications. The goal is to act in a way that meets all organizational standards and has the most positive impact on the employee's relationship with the supervisor. This can also be done effectively with status bars under each of these parameters for how in line the answers are with the organizational needs and the employee's happiness. For example, let's say there are two bars that go from 0-100 and they are both at 50 to start (Figure 7-1).

Figure 7-1. Status Bars

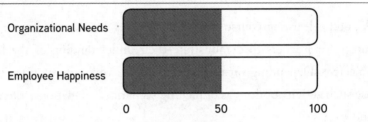

There may be an option that is best for the company, but destroys the relationship with the employee. So, the organizational score would increase, but the employee relationship score would decrease (Figure 7-2).

Figure 7-2. Status: Good for the Organization, Bad for the Employee Relationship

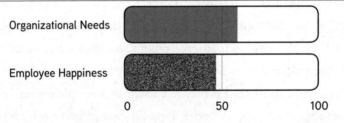

An option that is both good for the organization and the employee relationship might show small gains on both bars (Figure 7-3).

If you did something the employee liked but was ultimately a poor decision for the organization, the employee relationship bar would increase, but the organizational needs bar would decrease. And finally, you could make a decision that was bad for both the organization and the employee, which would lower both bars. This can be seen in action in the game *The Sims*.

Figure 7-3. Status: Good for Both the Organization and the Employee

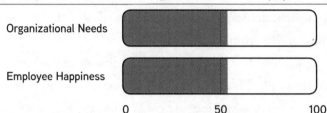

To differentiate this activity for learners' varying experience levels, you could provide an onscreen coach who offers suggestions for why one option would be better or worse than another. However, they would gain fewer points for a correct answer. That's because the time it would take to consult someone in real life would have an adverse effect on the employee's happiness. By that same token, learners would lose more points for an incorrect answer, because they consulted the coach and still got it wrong. These kinds of options help make the training content more nuanced, making it harder to simply guess the right answers. Learners' scores will thus reflect what they've learned.

Bear in mind that the more options that are provided in a branching scenario, the more time you'll spend in development. This is still the fastest of the suggested activities in this section, but it can become overwhelming. It is helpful to plan out branching scenarios with programs like Power-Point, or if you have a budget for it, something like BranchTrack.

Simulations

The second activity option is a simulation. With scenarios, learners were limited to a path to move through the course content. In a simulation, they have more possibilities for what they can do or how they can answer.

Simulations are commonly used in situations that require diagnosis or critical thinking. They are wonderful options for advanced learners dealing with complex issues. In the real world, what would you do if you really didn't know the answer? How would you troubleshoot fixing a car that is making a particular sound? How would you deal with a patient who is complaining of chest pain?

Let's think about how a simulation might work in our new supervisor training example. Instead of clicking on one of several answer choices to respond to the employee, learners could go to the employee handbook online, or speak to a member of the HR department, which could either be a chat bot or a branched scenario, before clicking back on the employee to move forward through the content.

When developing a simulation, remember that the order in which the learner selects options can affect the outcome. You'll need to not only develop a response for every choice a learner could make, but also consider every possible combination of things they could choose to do before that choice and what would happen. It's helpful to have lots of access to the SMEs to work through every combination of results and their implications. And you'll need time to code them all.

Interactions

A third option would be to show learners a series of interactions between a supervisor and employee. Have them rate the interactions on a scale of 1-5, with five being the best. For anything less than a five, provide feedback on why the organization agrees or disagrees with how the situation unfolded. After providing the feedback, describe how the interaction could be improved and why.

Next, you could ask learners to model the ideal behavior presented in the interaction and feedback. Give learners a scenario and have them record themselves. Allow them to review the video as many times as they'd like until they're comfortable with how they sound and their body language. Then ask them to give themselves a score and submit it to their coach or the SMEs who helped design the program. Repeat this process with several scenarios.

Games

A fourth option would be to create a game. Games get a lot of negative feedback from people outside of e-learning development because they think you want to have learners play a level of Tetris or Candy Crush as a thank you for doing well on the content. However, there are ways to create games that add value to learning and maintain engagement.

Good learning games incentivize learners to do something that reinforces the skills the course teaches. Does driving a race car down the street by typing faster add value? Yes, if you're teaching typing skills. In this case, the faster you type, the faster the car drives.

Similarly, if your goal is to help ensure that the learners know a series of new words, then building a crossword puzzle with definitions and synonyms as the clues would be an effective game. If the purpose of the course is to have learners use a fire extinguisher correctly, then a game where they have to do the steps in order to make the fire extinguisher work would be an effective game.

Consider a hospital that wants to prevent an infectious disease outbreak. Staff must learn to control infections before other patients and staff catch them. This could be presented as a game with rules based on hospital protocols for isolation, hand washing, and notifying the appropriate government organizations. If learners do tasks incorrectly or out of order, the disease will spread and they'll have to continue to try to contain it. At a certain point, too many people will become sick and they'll lose, or they will contain it and everyone will get better. Even if they win, learners will receive feedback at the end about whether they chose the right options in the right order or if they could have saved more people.

Games within the module aren't the only way to gamify e-learning. Another common gamification tactic is to have leaderboards with points where staff can compete with one another. Ensure that you have a good feel for the organization's environment before building something like this. In a collectivist organization, direct competition like this won't be popular. In an independent organization, it will likely factionalize into the people who compete hard for the highest scores and the people who are "actually doing their jobs" instead of spending time on training. It can be a very delicate, political balance to make that kind of board work well.

Your LMS may offer leaderboards, badging, and other gamification-type interactions. Again, consider this another tool in your toolbox—it is great to use in the correct application.

Games might not be feasible in organizations with limited resources or infrastructure. They also require quite a bit of technology. Just because your organization can support e-learning doesn't mean that your learners have access to computers or phones capable of competently navigating both the LMS and games embedded in the content.

Activity Benefits and Challenges

The best part of creating activities in e-learning is that you can provide instant, personalized feedback to learners. In the real world, it's unlikely that learners have their supervisors or coaches following them around giving them the feedback; even if this does happen, each supervisor has different experiences and different relationships with their employees. E-learning is different; experts can give learners perfect examples of the feedback that they want communicated about critical situations.

However, you may find it challenging to convince the SMEs to help you write feedback for when someone has made four or five of the worst decisions in a row. They might say, "No one would make decisions that horrible." In this case, you can bring up personas that may have difficulty with the content. Regardless of how a learner got to that place where they are, they'll want feedback to help them make better decisions, particularly if they are looped back to the beginning of the activity and have to take it again and again until they meet a measure of success required by the SME. You'll also want different feedback if someone chooses a poor first option and then gets the rest right, versus if they choose the first few correct and only miss the last one. The earlier in the scenario that they make a bad decision, the bigger its repercussions. Making a less than perfect initial decision, therefore, would be worse than making a less than perfect choice at the end of the scenario.

Another big challenge is collecting all the data to do the coding, and finding the time to develop scenarios and simulations where you don't think the learner will ever make such bad decisions. In real life, you would be able to respond in real time as learners make bad decisions and direct them back onto the appropriate course. In e-learning, unless you're giving feedback at each decision point, learners could go fairly far astray from what the organization would approve of in terms of behavior or choices.

Consider some expert advice on bargain feedback from Julie Dirksen, author of *Design for How People Learn,* on pages 91-94.

Bargain Feedback for Learning

Good feedback is a key part of a good learning experience. Learners can only get so far by consuming information; at some point, they need to try to *do* something, and get feedback on that action.

In an ideal world, learners would always have an expert coach standing right next to them giving them feedback on their attempts and helping them improve their next attempt. In the real world, that kind of coaching is usually cost prohibitive and logistically impossible.

So, what does a lower-cost version of good feedback look like? In a classroom environment, it can look like a learner attempting something in class and getting feedback from the facilitator, but even that model has its limitations. If an instructor has 30 learners, it can take up too much time to have each learner attempt the behavior and get feedback.

Here's where e-learning can come into play.

Automatic Feedback

You can have a computer provide feedback in the form of responses to multiple-choice questions. This is a limited option, however, and only helpful when you have well-defined rules for the actions. For example, procedures in healthcare or safety situations often have one right answer, but many other situations are more ambiguous. Is there a single "right" answer for how a manager should coach a failing employee, a teacher should talk to a bullied student, or a therapist should talk to a despairing client?

Self-Assessment

In the case of more ambiguous subjects, you can give people digital checklists or rubrics to self-evaluate. For example, you could have customer service representatives listen to recordings of themselves (or others) and evaluate those recordings based on a checklist of actions, or rubrics that allow them to judge for themselves how they did (Table 7-1).

Table 7-1. Sample Self-Assessment Rubric

Topic	Not Used	Beginner	Intermediate	Expert
Use of product knowledge	Did not reference relevant product at all	Mentioned the name of the relevant product	Was able to describe the main features of the relevant product	Was able to answer detailed product questions or describe how the relevant product meets the customer's need

Self-assessment can also take the form of comparing your response with one or more expert responses. For example, an e-learning training module on how to give constructive feedback to direct reports could look like the panels in Figure 7-4. Learners are given a scenario where they have to type their response (a). Then they have the opportunity to check or revise their answer based on a checklist (b). Finally, they can compare their answer with a few different examples from experienced managers, to see how experts would do it (c).

Figure 7-4. Feedback Scenario With Self-Assessment

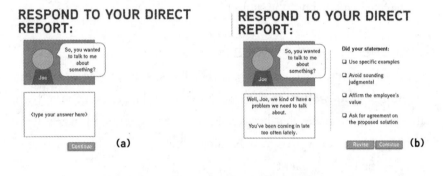

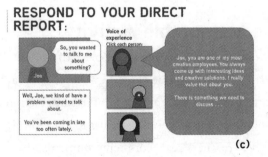

Peer-to-Peer Feedback

In a classroom, peer-to-peer feedback is relatively easy to organize—you can have people work in small groups and give one another feedback based on role plays or assigned tasks. In an online environment, however, peer-to-peer feedback is a little harder to organize, though not impossible. It can be done in an informal way, by making a discussion board available for people to share their work, or in a more formal and structured way, by matching people and giving them tools like a checklist or rubrics to facilitate feedback.

Several of the more successful MOOCs (massive open online courses) use peer-to-peer evaluation to allow for student feedback. Some students find the process of getting peer feedback valuable, but also learn a lot from being the person *giving* the feedback. The activity of evaluating others teaches them a lot about the subject.

The Challenge of Feedback

Feedback is often a challenge of scale. Feedback is easiest one-on-one, but learning solutions often need to work for much bigger audiences. There are still ways to make that happen. Many of them require learners to be active participants in their own learning, which can have benefits beyond any specific learning event.

Building a Memorable Activity

No modality is optimal for every person or piece of content. When developing activities, you should frame them in a variety of ways to allow all learners to connect with them. You'll hear about interaction being key to learner understanding, but it's more than just interaction. The interaction needs to connect to learners' real-world environments.

If you're creating supervisor training for people who work in an office space with cubicles, designing the e-learning course to look like that environment and having the people look like the staff will build stronger connections for learners and increase the likelihood that they'll apply the content on the job. If you're building supervisor training for people who work on a car assembly line, the same principle is in effect. You can take pictures of the work environment and the people to add authenticity.

An emotional connection to the content will also increase memorability and engagement. This can be done with case studies, whitepapers, or stories. While your learners won't meet with the SMEs directly when they take the e-learning course, this is still a great opportunity to share the SMEs' stories and experiences with them. There are reasons for the training they're receiving, usually stories based on what happened before this training was required. They are a strong way to connect back to the learners' "What's in it for me?"

Building for Your Audience

Practically speaking, start with the types of activities that your audience will react to positively. If your organization has a wiki where employees get information now, microlearning might be a better place to start than a multihour simulation.

Advice From the Trenches: JD Dillon

You can easily use simple design formats, such as pre-assessment and branching, within rapid development tools. This will ensure that employees consume only the content they need and that your course won't waste anyone's time. By acknowledging learners' current knowledge, you are demonstrating value while balancing the needs of the individual with the priorities of the business.

Consider the devices the learners have and the logistics involved with them taking training. If everything is done off the clock and while traveling, a mobile-compatible training course that allows for content acquisition in bursts will be a good choice. Learners' educational and linguistic backgrounds will also affect your development.

Embracing the Reality: Christopher Vella

How do you enable traditional sales representatives, who focus strictly on customer relationships, to embrace data-driven insights and thus increase follow-on sales? This was the challenge I faced when I started a project for a large life sciences company. I needed to develop a training program to teach sales reps the value of understanding customers' purchasing patterns to identify potential opportunities for additional sales. More technically, they had to learn how to use a collection of dashboards that aggregate information about their customers' purchases and the wide range of products the company sells.

After assessing what the organization and sales managers needed and profiling potential users, I set out to design a training program. It comprised five-minute videos that spent one minute explaining the purpose of a specific report, and then walked through a series of question and answer examples. I minimized the amount of audio and onscreen text so that people who don't speak English could use them. These videos were surprisingly popular around the globe.

Looking at the data you collected about the staff who will take the course and discussing with the SMEs the level of knowledge the learners have coming into this course will allow you to decide how best to develop to meet their needs.

How Many Activities?

A common question from new developers is how many activities should be included in a training course. This is a very narrow question due to the increasing flexibility for e-learning development, but in traditional e-learning, the recommendation is no more than four slides without learners having to do something. That something is more than clicking a Next button.

In practice, there's no hard and fast rule about the number of activities per minutes of content because the variety of activities that you can develop is so diverse the question wouldn't make sense. If your learners are in an interactive world where they have to click to make things happen, there's no additional activity that would need to happen to make it successful.

If you're not sure if you're going too light on activities, ask someone to take the training course with you, even if it's just as a storyboard. Talk them through what will happen and ask for their feedback on pacing. Most people will be able to give you an idea of what's working and what's not. Plus, if you're sitting there with them, you'll know exactly when it's been too long between interactions because you'll see their eyes glaze over.

Testing Activities

The great thing about activities is that you can generally test them apart from the content. You can develop them as paper games and have learners interact with them to find out what's working and what isn't. You don't need to give a whole lot of context once learners understand the parameters of the activity.

To test, start with a generic drawing or written explanation. The next round can include some graphic elements, but don't do something like the final version; the SMEs will get hung up on the look of the activity before the mechanics are ironed out. Once mechanics and content are approved, develop the final version and then let them see it for feedback.

Embracing the Reality: Nikki O'Keeffe

Behavior change on the job—isn't that the purpose of training? E-learning is training and should be more than a "tick the box" activity. An e-learning course that does not influence behavior change is a waste of everyone's time—designers, developers, and learners. Producing quality e-learning is an art and a technical process that requires multiple skills; it takes time. If it is rushed, quality will be compromised.

To do the final development, you'll want to use some type of digital tool. There are a number to choose from with a variety of unique features, so a combination of tools may best meet your needs.

SMEs are a great choice for providing quality assurance testing on activities because they'll go through the various options that they think are correct or not, and you can use their interactivity to tighten the feedback that they provided when the activity was more theoretical. When they go through it in the real world, other considerations may come into play that will cause them to want to make changes.

When reviewing activities, look out for:

- every option or combination having unique, specific feedback
- being able to go through the activity multiple times if the learner wants to (or has to) take it again without the previous answers showing up
- navigating forward and backward through the activity if the learner changes their mind in the middle of the activity
- good functionality in all the browsers and platforms that the learner may use.

Next

With the content laid out and the activities planned, it's time to develop the instructional materials. This is where you will choose the tools that you need to provide the content to your learners and receive feedback on how successful they were at accessing and understanding it. If you don't already know how you're going to develop this content, the next chapter will discuss the various reasons to go with specific authoring tools.

CHAPTER 8

E-Learning Authoring and Development Tools

If you've never developed e-learning before, authoring tools may be new to you. Most authoring tools are something like PowerPoint combined with a video editor. When you're beginning with an authoring tool, you can use it a lot like you would PowerPoint. There are slides where you can enter content. There are shapes for design, which you can make into buttons. You can type content onto the screen and animate it. You can sync audio. But why do you want or need an authoring tool?

Authoring tools offer a level of customization not available in Power-Point. Development for different size screens can be done quickly and easily in an authoring tool. These tools are a must-have for simultaneous, easy desktop and mobile development. They can also track user data.

If you're new to e-learning authoring and developing, it doesn't particularly matter which e-learning development tool you use. The way that most people choose to use one versus another is usually what they are taught in school or what an organization already uses. If you're able to choose, there are a few different considerations:

- **Cost.** The trend over the past few years is for the latest versions of major authoring tools to move to subscription models. The benefit of this is that you always have the latest software available, with the drawback being that you pay continuously for use. You may also have to pay for licenses for the reviewers in addition to the developers if you don't have another tool that meets that need. Fees can run from free for the tool H5P to $8,500 annually for SHIFT eLearning Enterprise. Many tools are around $1,300 annually per developer. If you work for a government or nonprofit organization, you might typically prefer owning software to paying regular licensing fees.

- **Usability.** The more comprehensive the authoring tool, the more features you have to learn to use. You'll have to decide whether you prioritize ease of use or the ability to customize.
- **Support.** If you're working alone, it's unlikely that other members of your organization will know how to use an e-learning authoring tool. Make sure you consider what support the vendor offers and the costs associated with it.
- **Output format.** This is another area where you need to confer with IT and determine how the final modules will be shared with learners. The output of the authoring tool will need to be acceptable to the LMS (or other sharing platform) as well as the assessment option that you want (AICC, SCORM 1.2, SCORM 2004, xAPI). Consider the way in which your learners will access the module. If you need to develop for desktop, mobile, and tablet access, do you want to develop the content three times, per language, to share it? Think about how much updating you'll have to do if you need to make changes. Several platforms offer you the ability to develop one time for multiple devices.

Advice From the Trenches

When I started at my company, I chose to use the tool that I learned while I earned a master's degree, given that the company had never used anything before and let me choose. At the time, the software had jumped several versions since my last use, so I had a bit of a learning curve for all the new features. I started developing and things went fairly well. Then my organization started partnering with other organizations that made e-learning courses and wanted me to make a few nominal, but important, content changes to the other organizations' content. Unfortunately, the other organizations used a different e-learning authoring tool. I then had to justify why I was using one tool rather than "what everyone else is using."

Lesson learned: Just because you may know one tool more than others doesn't mean it's the right fit for your organization. Take some time to assess whether there is an advantage to another tool. Or, find out if having several tools is an option. Each tool has a variety of tradeoffs that may make it better for a particular type of content or audience.

Choosing Your Tool

Looking at the four parameters mentioned, you can begin researching different tools. It's not worth it to write out the features of each authoring tool here; they're updated often enough that any issues at the time of publication will be resolved in future versions. There are several big-name authoring tools as of 2018, such as Adobe Captivate, Articulate Storyline 360, Elucidat, Gomo Learning, and Trivantis Lectora. Most tools offer a free trial; download them and kick the wheels. The learning curve for each varies significantly; the one you learn to use the fastest may not be the best solution for the type of development you're doing.

These software tools are a combination of desktop and cloud platforms. Keep in mind your Internet access, sharing, and individual features of each tool. Overall, these are more expensive tools, but each has a variety of features and benefits.

There are other tools that you can use for development as well, such as Adobe Premiere, Microsoft PowerPoint, TechSmith Camtasia, and TechSmith Jing. These tools are useful for specific purposes. The Adobe Creative Suite has a number of tools that complement development by allowing you to create and edit video, sound, vector images, raster images, and cartoons. You probably already have PowerPoint (so cost is not an issue), and you can use it to create graphics, charts, and tables.

Embracing the Reality: Nikki O'Keeffe

As you are creating your course, think about how you are going to manage authoring tool licenses and e-learning files. Could someone else easily step in to update your course? When only one person in an organization oversees the e-learning courses, it can be difficult for others to find, access, or edit course files when needed: "Oh, I know that [name] created that time management course. I am sure that you can grab the file from the network drive and make edits." User beware: If the previous person left the company, is on maternity leave, or has moved to another area of the business, those edits may not be so easy. I am sure we can all relate to similar scenarios.

When researching tools, don't think that you have to use one exclusively. A combination of tools can be useful to meet your needs.

For example, consider screen recording. Camtasia, Jing, and Captivate all have that feature, but Camtasia will allow more advanced editing of that content. Captivate will allow you to make it so the learner has to click to advance the screens. Jing is free and will allow you to post short videos to its server so that you can email them to others. Is one better than the other? Not necessarily. Each of them is useful for a specific purpose. If whatever tool you choose as your primary tool doesn't meet all your needs, consider looking for freeware or plug-ins that can address it.

Additional Considerations

Hypertext markup language (HTML) is the language of websites. Cascading style sheets (CSS) is the design and format of websites. When you export content from your e-learning authoring tool, the files that come out include HTML and CSS. While you don't have to edit these files in most circumstances, you can customize them before publishing to the Internet or your LMS.

JavaScript is the language that allows for interactive effects on websites. Knowing JavaScript will allow you to do some of the functionality in e-learning authoring tools more quickly than using the interface, and you'll be able to do more than the interface offers. Some tools support JavaScript while others do not.

If you'd like more advanced analytics or to connect your e-learning course to the outside world, consider learning about xAPI, one of the main languages for data collection. xAPI can be natively supported within e-learning authoring tools, or it can be added. Unlike JavaScript, not all LMSs support xAPI, so if this is something that you're considering, check your LMS. If it doesn't support xAPI, purchase a learning record store (LRS). An LRS is the database that stores the information about the interactions learners have with the training program and on the job.

Advice From the Trenches: Megan Torrance

Do you need more data to support your instructional design deliverables? Are you finding that your LMS is just not enough? You may be ready for xAPI, or the Experience API.

xAPI is an open specification for storing and retrieving records about learners and sharing those data across platforms. These records, known as activity statements, can be captured in a consistent format from any number of sources (learning record providers), and they are aggregated in a learning record store. The LRS is analogous to the SCORM database in an LMS, but doesn't do all the things that an LMS does.

The *X* in xAPI is short for *Experience* because the record providers could be anything we interact with, not just traditional AICC- and SCORM-based e-learning. With xAPI, you can track classroom activities, usage of performance support tools, participation in online communities, mentoring discussions, performance assessment, on-the-job activities and behaviors, and actual business results. All of this creates a full picture of an individual's learning experience and how that relates to their performance.

With xAPI, L&D teams will have much better data to support more advanced analytics, looking more deeply at the learning experience and the connection between learning and performance. Where do you start? This is often just as much a strategic and change management decision as it is a technology one. You can start with a big, high-visibility project or a small, under-the-radar one, depending on your situation.

Big strategic projects attract budget, resources, cross-functional collaboration, and scrutiny. When leadership says, "We're going to do this, and we're going to do this right!" that's often a clear call for enhanced data to support decision making. Simply knowing how many people completed an e-learning course may not be enough information. In this case, going big—setting up an LRS (because most LMS products are not running fully xAPI-ready environments), using xAPI-ready courseware development tools, building custom software to gather data outside of e-learning, and establishing a learning analytics environment—is the way to go. It's your chance to get the resources you need to get started, and the management attention to bust through roadblocks when they appear.

For big projects like this, L&D, IT, and the business are encouraged to work together, rather than stand at odds with one another. If you're a solo instructional designer, it's likely that a big xAPI implementation like this will be developed in partnership with vendors and your role will be that of "translator" in your organization.

As a solo instructional designer, taking smaller steps will help you build your case, learn as you go, and prepare your organization for a future xAPI implementation. As you're doing this, you learn who in the organization has the data and connections you need, how to navigate your single sign-on environment (or lack thereof), and how best to structure activity statements to get the best information out later on in their reporting. Enlist the support of your IT team and your project sponsors. Without a big, splashy announcement, you will be able to leverage the power of xAPI to get better data and make better decisions.

Getting Started With the Authoring Tool

The most important thing you can do when you start with a new tool is spend as much time as possible using it. A low-pressure way to do this is to develop lots of smaller modules to get used to the functionality. The Articulate community has weekly e-learning challenges where you can submit and get feedback from other developers. Even if you aren't comfortable submitting for yourself, you can review previous challenges and try to replicate them.

Doing this outside the projects you're completing for work will give you the opportunity to fail and receive feedback from other developers. Or, if you happen to be a quick learner and become an amazing developer doing cutting-edge development, you'll win the challenge for the week.

With your content and your tools in hand, consider the audio, graphics, and videos you'll need to create your training program.

The Learning Management System

One type of tool that hasn't been discussed is the authoring tool embedded in the LMS. The nice thing about using these tools is that you know it will be compatible with the way that you share it. It makes it easy to update and keeps the content with the distribution system.

If you decide to go this way, which can be compelling, make sure you find out what happens with the content in the event you choose to move to another LMS. Will your files be compatible with another system? Is there a way to export them?

Should you switch LMS providers, bear in mind you'll be learning a new authoring tool in addition to a new LMS administration tool.

Buying an LMS

If your organization is brand new to e-learning, you may now find yourself in a situation where you need to find or purchase a distribution system for your modules. Typically this will be an LMS.

As with the modules, this process will begin with a needs assessment to determine functionality and the users. As a department of one, you don't have time to act as the administrator. This is a situation where paying for an organization to customize and maintain the LMS might be in your best interest.

Costs for the LMS generally include a setup fee, which can be several thousand dollars, and then a cost per person per year. Typically, initial contracts are for three years.

You should consider how your ideal LMS will connect to your HR system or other talent management systems. That will enable the LMS to generate and disable accounts as quickly as your organization gains or loses them. It will also allow for job transfers to automate course assignment based on those changes.

There are LMS programs that you can purchase and host that will require more setup and administration on your part. The benefit to these is that they allow you to pay an up-front cost and then no additional licensing. An example is the WordPress plug-in LearnDash.

If your budget doesn't allow you to buy the LMS outright, there are a number of open-source options to consider. Examples include Moodle, Blackboard, and Sakai.

If the organization will use xAPI, it will also need a learning record store, or LRS. Most current learning management systems do not include this natively, so you can purchase plug-ins or use a separate system that you combine with the LMS via a dashboard.

LMS Alternatives

Why consider an LMS? Well, if you need to have logins to be able to track who is taking each course and manage long-term course scores, then an LMS is your best bet. If this isn't a concern, you have lots of flexibility in how you share your content:

- **Option 1: Company intranet.** If your company uses SharePoint or another intranet, you can add your training modules here.

Because it's an intranet, you'll know that the only viewers are members of your staff.

- **Option 2: Google apps.** Some organizations have made really beautiful microlearning apps with free features available in Google apps. You can create websites and link them into individual apps. They'll be easily compatible with Android devices and still provide general analytics.

- **Option 3: Selling through an e-learning website.** There are a number of reselling organizations for e-learning content. You can license it to organizations or individuals. One of the most common sites for this is Udemy. LinkedIn Learning offers corporate accounts that allow you to view their content and then add your own content just for yourself.

Next

Now that you've figured out which tools are at your disposal to create and share the content with your learners, it's time to see how you can weave multimedia options such as audio (chapter 9) and graphics and video (chapter 10) into your e-learning programs.

CHAPTER 9

Audio

One benefit to audio for e-learning is that you create an additional channel for content comprehension. If you have complex content onscreen, allowing learners to hear the explanation rather than read and watch it at the same time will allow them to acquire and understand it more quickly.

Think about learning how an engine works. The onscreen visual could be a picture of an engine with various parts highlighted, or a video of a real engine running. If the learner has to understand what's happening, showing it as text onscreen will detract from the images also on the screen. The first level of audio might be the sound of the engine. The sound is a useful addition, especially if learners can use it to diagnose a problem with the engine. Secondly, having a voice explaining the function or issue allows learners to focus on the imagery.

The first step is to determine whether audio is a value-add for the project you're completing. This should be done in the needs assessment. While having audio adds a channel for learning, does it make sense for the audience? How will learners access the content? Sometimes learners will take training on their desktop computers, which don't always have speakers. They would need to be provided with speakers or headphones. Additionally, can learners wear headphones on the job—for example, if it's a training course on a mobile device? These are things worth considering as you go into development.

Bear in mind the frequency of updates to the content as well. If minor changes will happen continuously, text-to-speech is by far the least expensive option for maintenance.

Assuming that you've determined that you do need audio, let's look into other considerations. A lot will be forgiven if the audio quality is good, but no amount of beautiful visuals can make up for a module with bad audio. If it comes down to bad audio or no audio, choose no audio. To that end, do you want to deal with audio production?

Considerations for Text-to-Speech

The value of text-to-speech (TTS) is speed. As fast as you can copy and paste your script into the software you use, whether it's the operating system's built-in function or Adobe Captivate, you'll have the audio files you need. If the name of your product changes, simply type in the new name and export the audio again. No audio editing, and no background noise.

But, it's a computer reading the content. That means that it lacks the human connection. Your learners will lose interest much faster with text-to-speech than they will listening to another person. You also have to keep in mind the language level of the content and the learners. If you're doing medical training with lots of technical disease or chemical names, the text-to-speech will be far less accurate than a human voice. You can manage this in several text-to-speech applications by using the phonetic alphabet, but it is very time consuming to get the inflection and pronunciation perfect. If your learners are taking the module in a language that is not their first, text-to-speech will be harder for them to understand.

Text-to-speech continues to sound more and more like an actual human voice (think Amazon's Alexa and Apple's Siri), but we're a few years away from a voice that can realistically modulate the way a real person's voice does.

Also keep accents in mind. Many programs now offer several portrayals of English, with varying U.S., British, Australian, and South African accents. These countries have a variety of accents; the accent of a New Yorker, for instance, is significantly different from that of an Oregonian. Whenever possible, have a native speaker of the language confirm the accent you think you're using with the audience against the finished audio file. It is common for the wrong country to be associated with the text-to-speech voice.

As a department of one, you need to weigh the benefits of a human actor's feeling and modulation against the time to record, time to edit, cost of materials, learning curve of the software, and location. Almost all of these can be managed with the use of good text-to-speech software.

Appropriate Uses for TTS

Regardless of what your final product will be, text-to-speech is invaluable as placeholder text for the review cycle. If the final version will have professional audio, use the text-to-speech to get approval from the SMEs and your sponsor.

Text-to-speech continues to improve to the point that it will likely pass the Turing test within the decade. When that happens, e-learning developers will be able to use TTS without having to go through the expense and time of recording a human.

Embracing the Reality

In my first few months at a new company in my department of one, I created storyboards and sent them to the SMEs for review and approval. I thought it worked well because I received the storyboards back with edits. Then I created about half a dozen modules and asked for final sign off. To my surprise, I received extensive changes. Understanding that this was suboptimal for future development, during the next round of review, I met with each SME individually after sending them the storyboard. We discussed changes face-to-face. The last person I met with had the benefit of all the suggestions from the other SMEs. I found that I had to go back through the first SMEs to review the feedback from the later experts. To combat this, with the next storyboard, I brought the SMEs together and projected the storyboard so they could all see it, and then read the voice-over out loud. Their ability to hear me interact with the content allowed them to get a better feel for how the final product would sound and made it easier to "hear" the voice-over so they could offer more productive feedback. Because I also was the actor for the modules, they knew exactly what it would sound like for the learners.

Now I have this storyboarding reading session to get approval on the final storyboard round before I go to development in the e-learning authoring tool.

Text-to-Speech Providers

Both Apple and Windows operating systems have voices build into their interface. The software you use to develop your e-learning module can access these voices and read the content. Apple OS will allow you to save any text on your computer as an iTunes file that can be added to other programs as well.

Adobe Captivate and Articulate Storyline have several additional integrated voices that can be accessed for this purpose.

Other voices can be purchased from a variety of online vendors to add additional languages and accents. When researching one of these for your use, ensure that you determine the pricing structure. Some organizations charge on a per-syllable basis, while others charge per word.

Professional Actors or Amateur Talent?

If you want to have real people record the audio for your module, you can use professional voice artists or amateurs. There are advantages and disadvantages to each (Table 9-1).

Professional Actors

A professional actor will be the most expensive, but in terms of time, they'll have the least impact on your schedule. Using your hourly rate, work out how much it will cost you to edit the audio files discussed in the next two sections, and multiply the cost by three times the length of time it takes to play the audio. That's the minimum cost for you to do the editing. If a professional actor will cost less, choose them!

Ensure you meet any legal requirements for your organization and the actor for continued use of their voice in current and future modules, with editing, for potential financial gain. If possible, also build into the contract for the actor to record future changes.

Table 9-1. Advantages and Disadvantages of Using Professional Actors

Advantages	Disadvantages
• Will either have their own recording studio or know where they can go to record	• Potential additional cost to rent the studio space for the recording
• Professional-grade studio will provide good levels and usable files	• Pay for voice-over every time you record (not building corporate value)
• Option to do basic editing	• Additional fee for more advanced editing
• Takes less time for a professional actor to record content than someone inexperienced	• You have to pay the professional voice actor
• Requires less of your time because you won't have to manage the software, recording, or direction	• Actor may not say things exactly how you'd like if you don't supervise

Co-Workers, Friends, and Family Members

Co-workers will likely be very excited to do something different on the job by acting as "talent" for your department. Make sure you check with HR to have the employee sign any paperwork to allow their voice (and image) to be used even after they've left the company. Table 9-2 has some advantages and disadvantages of using amateur talent.

Embracing the Reality

I attended a training session to watch a SME present on a new topic. She was the voice talent for a previous module, and I am the voice talent for many of the modules. I generally sit in the back of the room and take notes but don't talk to the learners to get an understanding of their questions. At the end, I went up to ask the SME a few questions and a learner who was lingering ran up excitedly asking why she felt like she knew us. We listed off a few titles in which we performed and the learner was thrilled. She even asked for our autographs and told other employees that she met the people behind the training.

It was an incredibly sweet moment for the SME to be recognized and associated with the content that she'd developed even though she hadn't gotten to present the entry-level class to the learner. She definitely understands the value of voice-over now; as more modules are created, she'll do a small part of the audio so staff know who she is when they meet her later. It's also nice as the developer to be recognized when you seldom get away from the computer.

Table 9-2. Advantages and Disadvantages of Using Amateur Talent

Advantages	Disadvantages
• Inexpensive to build a functional studio	• Additional cost to rent or build a recording studio space
• You will learn recording software	• Cost of recording software, cost of recording materials, space for recording
• You will learn audio editing	• Time to learn recording software, time to learn audio editing best practices
• Inexpensive or free talent	• Training time for talent • Time to edit multiple takes • Lots of supervision
• Diversity of voices, accents, and genders	• Usually takes longer to record than recording yourself

Recording Yourself

You'll have all the same advantages of using co-workers, friends, and family members but with the convenience of knowing when you can record yourself. Scheduling can only be easier than doing it yourself by using text-to-speech.

A drawback to consider is that you'll have to listen to your own voice. Because you hear your voice in your head, it sounds deeper to you when you speak than it does in a recording. Many people find it difficult to listen to themselves. Especially in the beginning, you'll be going through lots of rounds of editing, so you want to keep that in mind.

For co-workers, friends, family members, and yourself, you'll need to consider the audio equipment.

Recording Equipment

Recording studios are amazing when you have access to them and a budget to use one. Typically it's an hourly cost to use the room, plus the cost of a sound technician. Unless you're using a professional actor, you should factor in the time cost of the recording session as well.

Building a recording studio at your office can be less expensive than you think. If you have a room that you can use, it's a matter of a few packing or shipping blankets, a table, and a good microphone. If you don't have a room to use, you can hang blankets around the microphone in a cube or tent shape. Barring that, you can make a desktop-size box and put a microphone inside that. Keep in mind that the size of the space dramatically affects the way the voice sounds. You can tell if a person is recorded in an opera house or a closet regardless of the microphone quality.

The biggest expense will be purchasing a quality microphone. Spend what you can to get the best microphone based on research from e-learning and podcasting sources. Whenever possible, purchase several, record the same content on all of them, and listen to the quality differences. Choose the one that sounds the best in your particular environment. Keep in mind the quality ratings. Does it matter if you have to replace the microphone every year? Do you want to have one microphone that will last for several years?

Make sure to also purchase a pop blocker. This will save editing time by mitigating the plosive sound made when pronouncing *p* and *b* noises.

Thankfully, once you've purchased the microphone and blocker and set up a space, there is no additional cost for more recordings.

Background Sounds and Music

Adding a bit of music to the intro or outro can help set the tone or convey the consistent corporate introduction. Light background music can create an enjoyable ambience, but will add to the cognitive load for your learner. Determine the level of difficulty of the content and ensure that you aren't adding music that will adversely affect the content acquisition.

Background sounds can be useful for setting the stage for the content. If you're doing a management training program in a retail environment, it might be helpful to have the sounds of the store and cash registers in the background during scenarios to imitate the real-life experience.

Music can be a useful tool when the audio is inconsistently recorded. If you have to piece together audio from different sources, taped at different times, or with background noise that you can't remove, music can make the content audio seem more level.

If you have the time and inclination, you can create your own audio using GarageBand. Either record the ambient sound from the work environment or mix together audio using clips. There are lists of websites with free music available for Creative Commons licensing. If you're selling the module, purchase the appropriate level of rights for distribution.

Audio Editing and File Storage

The program used to record the audio will determine the ease of editing and file storage.

If you record directly into your authoring software (Captivate, Storyline), the audio will be recorded a slide at a time. This is a positive in that you can see the closed captioning as you do the editing and each file is small. The authoring software will dictate the size and the storage location within the project library.

The difficulty with this method is the time it takes to record and maintain the consistency between the individual audio files. You'll have to start and stop multiple times. If you have a co-worker or an actor standing there waiting while you click at least three times each time they can record, they may get frustrated. It's also hard for them to get a flow and speak normally because everything is broken into little bits. If you're recording to cover multiple slides, it's slightly more complicated to adjust this after the fact when recording directly into the authoring tool. If you're recording yourself, you may not reset to the same distance from the microphone because you're moving back and forth between the recording setup and the computer screen, causing the volume to be lower or higher. As far as the consistency between files, not only do you have the volume and tone differences of the voice-over person, but if the room has a steady background noise, like an air conditioner, you will need to edit this out from each file individually.

The other option is to record all the audio in a single file with an external program, such as Audacity or Audition. There are several benefits here, including your ability to remove all background noise and do leveling once for the entire file. If you do nondestructive editing, you also will always have the file if something happens within your authoring file. That means, if you keep the original file of the raw audio, you can make edits on a copy file so that if you don't like something you've done, you can go back to the original. This is much harder to do in the authoring tool. If you are recording someone other than yourself, another benefit to this way of recording is how much time it saves for your talent. They simply read the entirety of the script, however many times you'd like, and they can leave. They don't need to wait for you to start and stop as you advance from slide to slide.

The drawback here is file maintenance and editing time. You'll first need to determine the file type for recording. You can go from completely uncompressed (WAV) to highly compressed (MP3 or AVI). As a classical musician, I can hear the difference in compression rates in classical music. For talking, this is much less obvious, so sound can be highly compressed and a person skilled in audio won't notice it as much. Generally, you want to minimize the size of your overall presentation to make it easier to download, so you'll choose the highest level of compression that doesn't adversely affect the quality (to the level a learner would notice it) and keep it as small as possible.

Once you've selected it, you then need to set up a location to save the files. If you use Captivate, the My Adobe Captivate Projects is a useful place that already includes all of the Captivate files. Create a folder for the project and build asset folders for the graphics, videos, and audio. Then subdivide the audio in the background sounds, if any, and each language of the content.

Keep the original audio file. Duplicate it and use that for editing in case anything should happen. Apply the major edits over the entire file, and then cut into the content for each slide. Save the files in the same folder and then add them to the library file in the authoring tool.

Overall, audio is a valuable addition to e-learning development, but it is time intensive and potentially costly. You will need to ensure the value of it for the final module because it will be a significant time investment for you. However you choose to store your materials, make sure you have a plan to back up your files! There's nothing worse than having to hire an actor to come in because you accidentally lost everything. I've done it and they aren't happy about it! I now have a backup drive I connect to each evening that mirrors my computer.

Next

While audio on its own can have tremendous value, as the expression goes, a picture is worth a thousand words. Developing or curating pictures and video will build engagement for the learners of your content. The next chapter covers best practices in creating graphics and videos for e-learning.

CHAPTER 10

Graphics and Video

If you've developed the most compelling content ever written but then present it as text on slides, it won't matter how good it is; your learners will be unenthusiastic about finishing it. You can do some interesting animations with text, but they won't carry a long presentation.

Graphics and video break up content blocks and can improve learners' ability to understand and retain the content. Think about building a module to train supervisors on having difficult conversations with staff. You could model these conversations for learners in a few ways.

A first option would be including a text bubble on each side of the slide; the bubble text would match the voice-over. You'll have to make it clear that this is a face-to-face conversation and not texting, however, which may be difficult because that's how the conversation would be shown (Figure 10-1).

Second, you could have a static image of a person on either side of the screen. When one person is talking, you can gray out the other person to make it obvious who is speaking. Or, use each slide for one text bubble, to indicate that the conversation goes back and forth between the characters and learners have to do something to advance the conversation (Figure 10-2).

Figure 10-1. Option 1 for Modeling Difficult Conversations

Figure 10-2. Option 2 for Modeling Difficult Conversations

Image courtesy of eLearning Brothers

A third option would be to animate the characters in a scene, so the action flows back and forth between the two characters. The benefit of this style is that it appears organic and allows learners to feel as if they're watching the situation. Using animation for this interaction also makes it less confrontational than using real people (Figure 10-3).

Figure 10-3. Option 3 for Modeling Difficult Conversations

Image courtesy of eLearning Brothers

Finally, you could videotape the scene between two co-workers or actors. This is the most realistic experience for learners and will show subtle facial expressions and reactions.

Each of these options has pluses and minuses in how it's learned, how much time it will take, and how much it will cost. The rest of this chapter will walk you through making those determinations as a department of one.

Graphics

It will be beneficial for you to build your graphic design skills if you don't have them already. Developing your own graphics allows you to make training look much like what learners experience in real life, and can help them connect what they learn to their jobs. It can be less expensive in terms of direct costs, but you should keep a log of how long you spend building and editing graphics to see how much of your time it takes.

Regardless of whether you have a background in graphic design, here are a couple considerations to keep in mind when attempting to spruce up your e-learning: whether to use photographs or illustrations, and whether (and how much) to pay for graphics or use free resources.

Photographs vs. Illustrations

Your fellow staff can be an excellent resource for models to illustrate what you're trying to teach in your modules. If what you're training on is easily captured in a photo, you can snap photos of colleagues doing the job to support any text.

However, if you're not on-site for where training might be used, you could obtain a green screen (or tape green paper or cloth to the wall) and have your staff stand in front of it in a variety of different positions. Then, you can overlay them onto other photos at the work site. The green cloth or paper may cost you $20 or so but will save countless hours on the computer, because you can use the color remover feature. Just ask your staff not to wear green clothes!

Be careful when editing these photos. Changing the way people look can be seen as offensive. The best option is to light people as well as possible, do basic color correction, and send the photos to the employees for approval. Some employees will want to look exactly as they do in real life. Others will ask for more editing. Regardless of what they request, all changes should be driven by the employee and you should not make any edits without their written request.

When it is impractical to use actual photographs of a scene, changing the photograph to an illustration is a viable option. This can be done in a variety of ways. Photographs can be imported into Photoshop, or Power-Point in a pinch, and shapes can be superimposed over them to make an illustrated version of the photograph. Figure 10-4 shows an illustration that was created in Photoshop.

Figure 10-4. Example of a Photograph Transformed Into an Illustration

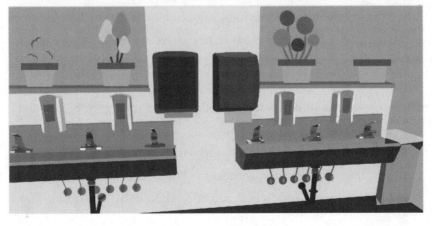

Illustrations can be helpful for two reasons. First, you may need to simplify the scene to make it easier to focus on what's important. In Figure 10-4, cabinets in the background on the far wall were removed. Because the focus of the module was handwashing techniques, learners were able to focus on the items of interest in the foreground, which were easier to see in the illustration. The main focus of the illustration is the two sinks, the soap dispensers, and the paper towel dispensers.

Second, the training course may deal with uncomfortable topics where having softer, less realistic images will make it easier to deal with the content. In the difficult conversations topic example, learners are much more likely to focus on the content of the topic than the people if they don't already know them. You can also add distance between the content and the characters by making them nonhuman or colors that are not associated with skin tones, like blue or green.

To give another example, Figure 10-4 is part of a module that explains the spread of bacteria, told from the perspective of a bacterium in a classroom. This perspective makes the concept of handwashing more engaging and interesting.

Paid vs. Free Graphics

If you're considering paid graphics, you can look into purchasing a stock art subscription. Numerous organizations have started to fill this gap for e-learning developers; the two biggest are eLearning Art and eLearning Brothers. Both have a variety of photorealistic and cartoon-style images. Their costs vary and both offer several packages to meet your individual needs.

Or, you can purchase individual images from typical stock artwork organizations. If you find yourself using lots of photographs or illustrations, you might consider purchasing a bulk subscription to keep costs down. Check with your organization's content or marketing department—they might already have a subscription.

If you want to use free images, many e-learning blogs will provide annual lists of free graphics, audio, and video. In chapter 14, look at the recommended blogs and subscribe to the ones who will offer the content that's of most interest to you.

If you are selling your modules, be particularly careful if you are looking at Creative Commons licenses. Creative Commons is a copyright license that allows people to share materials that would normally require licensing fees. Typically, if you make money off the modules, you're unable to use Creative Commons images.

Video

Creating video can seem like a quick way to get instructional content to learners. Having the SME sit in front of a camera and recording their discussion on a particular topic can be useful for development if you won't have regular access to them and you want to have a resource for content details and the SME's speaking style. It can be tempting to do something like this for training staff, but in the industry, the somewhat negative shorthand for this type of training is "the talking head." You can use video of the subject matter expert talking about their subject, but do so sparingly to maximize learner interest.

In many ways, video is the only way to teach something that's not ridiculously expensive. Consider anything hands-on that you'd be expected to replicate: baking, pottery, knitting, playing an instrument. If you're a medical student who needs to learn how to remove an appendix, what better way to start learning how to do that than to watch lots of surgeries? This could be replicated with simulations, but would be prohibitively expensive and time consuming for a department of one.

Recording Your Own Video

This is a compelling option because it gives the perception of saving time. There is some truth to that when you're writing the script because you have the ability to ask questions, particularly if you're recording the subject matter expert on camera. Unfortunately, being less well scripted going into the recording means more time for video editing.

If you have a solid script and storyboard, recording videos has numerous benefits. Using other staff members for the recording will help the video be truly reflective of your environment, which can be hard to do with still graphics or animations.

Embracing the Reality: Anne Parmeter

After bouncing around doing training design for multinational corporations, I found an instructional design position for a nonprofit company. I remember asking my new manager about the budget for hiring a calligrapher and a musician for an e-learning course that I had designed, resources that I'd had at my disposal in previous jobs. She sat across from me on a sofa nodding thoughtfully, like an empathetic therapist with only questions and no solutions: "Let's see what you can do on your own, with what you have."

I likened the experience of sharing my early training videos with parading down the street naked. I was so uneasy and out of my element, afraid that everyone would know that I had no right to be handling a camera. But with each progressive video project, there was a glimmer of something a little bit great. People around the office seemed to think that my crappy hand-lettered videos and quirky humor were clever and fun. Gradually I developed my style and embraced things being handmade and charmingly low-tech. This scrappy style I had developed mirrored the pioneering way that the company had started, leveraging passion in place of material resources.

I am now a full-fledged one-woman training-video production studio, and I wouldn't have it any other way. I have probably developed about a hundred e-learning courses and videos for this nonprofit in the years since I joined the organization. What started with an iPhone and countless YouTube tutorials has morphed into stop-motion animation, live webinars, and extra revenue streams for the company.

For anyone out there wondering if you can create training videos with minimal resources, give it a shot. Fail successively as you move in a direction that feels honest and authentic.

The drawback to that is the level of detail in the frame. If the employee wears something that doesn't work, or you see something in the background in review that can't be shown, you have to rerecord the whole thing.

It also requires you to purchase quite a bit of equipment. At a minimum, you need a computer with a processor capable of running video-editing software, a decent video camera, a microphone, and several lights. See what exists elsewhere in your organization and use any available resources.

Advice From the Trenches

Working on a project to explain how to fill out some paperwork, I recorded an employee walking through the process in a conference room. There was great natural light and I brought in some additional lights. I coached the employee to wear royal blue, which would look good on camera. The day of the recording, she came in and had done her hair and makeup and was ready to go. I sat her in front of the wall and we moved the angle around a few different directions to find one that looked good for her. We recorded the session.

In post-production, I realized that several angles showed the door handle wall protector behind her. I thought I'd change the background to something else in all the frames to remove it. I tried several different background-removing programs, but with her blonde hair against a nude brown wall, I couldn't do it without removing part of her hair and or face.

That was the last time I recorded a talking head–type video without using a backdrop.

Consider the Timeline

Here's an example of the timeline to produce a project. The HR department thought it would be nice to have a bilingual keynote address to kick off a company-wide training. The e-learning developer blocked off two solid months to make what ended up being a nine-minute final project. She spent three weeks writing the script, inviting staff to participate, and scouting locations. In week four, the developer recorded the main part of the presentation. She spent week five editing the main part and then doing the supplemental interviews. During week six, the developer showed the rough cut to HR to get their feedback and approval. At the end of the week, she sent it for translation into Spanish.

Initially they planned for the onscreen text to be in the opposite language of the speaker, so when the employee was speaking in Spanish, the onscreen text would be in English. When the employee was speaking in English, the onscreen text would be in Spanish. Then in testing an employee inquired about the accessibility of the content in her language because she was hearing impaired. So, the developer changed the plan and put full closed captioning in both languages.

The editor spent week seven doing color correction to make all the clips look good together. She conducted three rounds of beta testing on staff to ensure that the content made sense. She also scouted the largest of the company training locations to see what the rooms looked like and what kind of multimedia offerings they had. Everything looked good.

Week eight was the company training. It took 320 hours of work to create and distribute a nine-minute video. You probably won't be able to block off two months for one project, so be sure to set timeline expectations with the stakeholders.

Internet Video

People love sharing their expertise with others. There's hardly a subject for which you can't find a video on the Internet. Many people are also happy to let you use their videos, often for free, with permission.

This allows you to curate content quickly and cheaply. The main drawback to this is if the author takes the video down, you lose your content.

Whenever possible, ask the original poster if they would be willing to provide the file to you for your own hosting.

Video Cartoon Animations

Introducing cartoons into the corporate environment can be a mixed experience. Some organizations don't like them because they see them as unprofessional. This does not have to be the case. There are plenty of uses for cartoons in a professional setting. Cartoons can be used to inject humor into training. When training on something important but not interesting, like the value of handwashing, using a cartoon to talk about the transfer of bacteria from hands to doorknobs to mouths and causing sickness is less gross when done as a funny cartoon than as a serious video.

There is some great software out there to quickly build video animations. GoAnimate allows you to create characters of varying ages and ethnicities and have them perform actions and speak. The beauty of video animations is your ability to control literally all parts of the frame. Unlike using real actors, you have complete control of every gesture, facial expression, and pose. You also write the words that they speak, and you can use either real voices or text-to-speech.

One of the benefits of cartoon animations is that you don't need other people in order to do the production; it can be done any time of day. It can also happen in any location. With cartoons, it could be in an office, outdoors, on a blank background, or in space.

Video Whiteboard Animations

Whiteboard-style videos make it look like someone is drawing on a dry-erase board and erasing it as the slides progress. This is a fun progression from cartoons that has animation and text. The limited color palette and simplistic style make it easy to adapt for a variety of cultures. Whiteboard animations are often used to teach things in a classroom style. A hand will write something on the slide and then erase it and then write the next lines. This is often seen in simple explainer videos that teach learners about a particular concept.

Writing Scripts

With any type of video, prepare to spend the most time in storyboarding and script writing. Having a clear direction going into the video production will dramatically reduce the time spent in the actual recording, and even more so in post-production.

Even with a SME who is highly knowledgeable on the topic and able to speak about it in meetings may not do as well on camera. On several occasions, even with bulleted scripts, SMEs have frozen in front of the camera. Lots of prep, explaining the situation, and a strong script can go a long way toward a good final product.

Embracing the Reality: Jonathan Halls

We've all heard Benjamin Franklin's line, "Those who fail to plan, plan to fail." And as much as it seems obvious and sage advice, it's easy to forget under the shadow of a looming deadline.

I've earned my bread and butter in the media industry for decades as a journalist, talk show host, media executive, and media trainer. All my successes come from the fact that I was taught by wise professionals.

One radio veteran shared a piece of wisdom with me in a scriptwriting class in 1990 that I'll never forget. "The best ad libs, Jonathan," he said, "are scripted." He could have been quoting Ben Franklin.

There are many good reasons for working off a written script. For one thing, it frees your mind to focus on your delivery. And a good script ensures that your words are focused, and there's no waffle. In other words, a script is a plan for you to sound really polished. Some people say a script makes you sound stilted, but I think it's a poorly written script that makes people sound wooden.

It's easy to think that we can create awesome digital content by winging it, whether it's a podcast, video, or written content. Sometimes we can. But most of the time we just set ourselves up for mediocre results, when a little planning can lead to better results.

When writing a script, start with a brainstorm or map of all the content you want to cover. Then organize the content so it flows between topics. From there, write it out like it's a conversation.

Remember that since this is e-learning, there will be onscreen content. You want action to drive the "conversation": If you can show it instead of saying it, do that. No one wants to read or listen to long paragraphs of text. Whenever possible, have learners interact with the content, followed by demonstrating the content, with the least time spent explaining content. Obviously this will vary with learners' experience with the content. The more knowledgeable they are, the faster the course can set them loose working through content. The less they know, the more context you need to provide to make them successful. With novice learners, consider offering optional supports they can turn on as required based on where they are in the content. If they need help, it's there, but it's not mandatory. Remember that experiencing content is the best way to learn it.

Planning for Your Recording

Now that you have a script and actors set up for the shoot, it's time to record. You need the following:

- ❑ confirmation of the location access and liaison
- ❑ list of all the equipment to bring
- ❑ several copies of the script, along with pencils and pens
- ❑ contact numbers for all the staff involved
- ❑ lights
- ❑ a camera
- ❑ a tripod

❑ extra batteries

❑ extra light bulbs

❑ the actors, each with at least one change of clothes

❑ enough materials to record the same shoot three times

❑ dots for marks on the walls or floors

❑ tape.

Recording day will probably be one of the few times that all your co-workers are interested in what you're doing. It's a great time to recruit someone to come as your shoot assistant. They can help set up all the lights, the camera, and anything that needs to be changed in the background. It can be useful if the person helping you is the same height as the SME, or whomever else you're taping, to use them for setting the lights.

Consider learning about documentary filmmaking to help you make the actors feel comfortable onscreen. If you're using professional actors, this is less of a concern, but with your co-workers, making them feel at ease in front of the camera will build rapport and help them feel and look good.

Talk with your actors about what you'll be recording and tell stories or jokes to keep the mood light. Have the actor speak to you, not to the camera, while they're being recorded. Look directly at them with as rapt attention as you're able. Take deep, regular breaths to have them mirror what you're doing and relax. If they're having a hard time sticking to the script, try guiding them through the content by asking them to answer questions by including the question in their answer. For example, they would answer, "What is the value of handwashing?" by saying, "The value of handwashing is the reduction of the spread of germs." If you need to go this route, work with them to leave space so that you can cut your voice out of the video.

Advice From the Trenches: Jonathan Halls

Shooting video in today's workplace can involve a lot of people, and all it takes is one person who drops the ball to make production time twice as long.

One of my clients was a Fortune 500 company that prioritized video to train staff at its retail service locations around the country. To make the instructional videos more authentic and familiar, the training director decided we should film them at store locations rather than in our makeshift studio. So, one Thursday afternoon, we set up the cameras and lights in a New York retail office to shoot an instructional video about the company's corporate brand and how to instill its values in customer interactions. The presenter stood with some merchandising material displayed prominently behind her. The filming went well and our SME, the merchandising manager, was pleased.

After two hours on location to film the video and four hours of editing, the video was sent to the vice president of marketing as a courtesy before uploading it to the LMS. And the vice president canned it. It turns out the branding in the merchandising was not up-to-date. He demanded that the team go back and film it all over again with the correct merchandise in the background. This meant working late and into the weekend to reshoot and get it finished. If only our SME had taken notice; it was his job to pick these things up. But instead, he was caught in the excitement of video cameras and lights.

The moral to this story? I now draw up a step-by-step production process for filming. And the SME must sign off on visual details like this before we leave the location. If they don't, then we don't move on to the next step. And if there's a mistake and we have a heavy backlog of other projects, that project goes to the back of the queue.

Post-Production

Taking into account graphics and video, post-production will take an exceptional amount of time. If you have the budget, consider hiring freelancers, graphic designers, and video editors. More than doing the actual work, learning the software and editing best practices is a career unto itself.

If you don't have the money to hire someone, then plan for at least five times the amount of time it took to record the video as to edit it:

- **First round:** watching the video
- **Second round:** transcribing the video
- **Third round:** cutting the video down to the transcriptions

- **Fourth round:** reorganizing the video to the storyline
- **Fifth round:** color correcting, transitions, and titles.

Depending on the visibility and size of the final audience, I recommend several rounds of testing with the audience to ensure it meets their needs.

The last piece of editing before distributing the video is to add closed captioning to ensure that all staff can understand and enjoy your modules.

Next

Now that we've reviewed best practices for using audio, graphics, and video in your e-learning development, it's time to turn to ensuring that the training you're creating remains accessible to all your learners. By paying attention to legal requirements, education and language level, visual and auditory impairments, and learning disabilities, you can design e-learning that everyone can use.

CHAPTER 11

Accessibility

During your needs assessment, you will find out about the staff in your organization. It will be incumbent on you to develop content that all staff in your organization, or potential customers, will be able to use. While there is legislation for government entities, your company may not be under that jurisdiction. Simply because you are not currently expected to comply doesn't mean that you shouldn't develop to this level. There are a number of benefits to building with accessibility, such as ensuring that future learners will be able to take the training course if they need accessibility features and that you use best practices in your content development.

Education and Language Level

Learners' educational background and language level will determine the content's complexity and how to manage cognitive load. For example, when you have staff who are learning in a language other than their native one, you should consider how the content is being presented.

Considerations include:

- **How content is presented onscreen.** Large paragraphs of onscreen text are demotivating even for native-language readers but can be daunting when working in another language. How can you communicate the content with learners without writing it out? Even with native speakers, look back at the organizational needs assessment you conducted in chapter 1 and the Flesch reading level material to determine what staff are familiar with and able to understand.

- **When to use audio in addition to visual content.** One option is to include a voice-over in the module to decrease cognitive load by giving learners another channel by which to obtain information. The more complex the visuals, the greater the need for an audio explanation.
- **Closed captioning.** If you include audio in the presentation, it's important to have a closed captioning channel so that learners can view difficult words or get assistance with accents. It's particularly important when using text-to-speech because computer voices don't have the level of articulation that human voices do.

Think about the audience you have for supervisor training. If anyone in the organization who wants to and is approved by their supervisor can attend, then there likely won't be any education requirements beyond those for initial hiring at your organization. That may lead to high school graduates and PhD recipients alike taking the course. If that's the case, you'll need to consider if it's practical for you to develop different levels of the program to meet the Flesch score levels of each of those groups. You'll also need to consider which languages to generate for the training—and this may vary by module. If management is required to speak the main language of the organization, having them take most of the courses in that language makes sense. But it may be appropriate to offer technical information in additional languages.

Visual Impairments

As of 2015, 2.3 percent of U.S. adults, or approximately 7.3 million Americans, reported a visual disability (NFB 2018). This can encompass anything from color blindness to decreased ability to see to complete blindness. Designing training that better meets the needs of employees with visual impairments can improve the quality for all staff. The simplification of visual content that allows learners with visual impairments to understand it is also a best practice for developing for mobile devices.

Advice From the Trenches: Russ Stinehour

Creating accessible learning content is more than adhering to Section 508 standards. It's more than providing video closed captioning and screen-reader-friendly images and text. Learning content is not accessible until the learner says it is accessible. Difficulties with contrast, text size, color blindness, central vision loss, and peripheral sight limitations are a few of these learners' needs. These learners, known as "zoomers," face challenges in consuming content using these tools.

This does not mean that it is impossible to meet the various needs of this large and growing population. The best way to meet most of the assorted requirements is to simplify the learning work flow and provide a single task to the learning page. Designing for mobile devices first can give the designer a significant head start in doing this. Consistent placement of instructions, buttons, and other user interface widgets can greatly help. Crisp, easy to understand animations and simulations can help learners with low vision find and use the learning objects. Removing clutter and providing white space goes a long way in helping them find information and navigate learning content. Shortening the word count and list length can help make scrolling easier. Remember, if it is good design for these learners, it is even better design for sighted learners. When it comes to designing accessible learning content, the key is to get started and don't quit.

There are two main tools used by learners who are visually impaired: screen readers and magnification. A screen reader allows learners to hear the content on the screen. For this to work, you need to be developing with alt text. Alt text is something that was used more in lower-bandwidth times—it was the text describing the image that would load if you had the patience to wait it out. Developing with alt text is easy, albeit time consuming. If you're building conversation slides for an activity, if you build the first slide with alt text and then duplicate it, that description will stay from the previous slide and you can edit it as appropriate. If you're using new images on each slide, you'll need to add alt text for each image on each screen. Another positive of developing with the accessibility mentality is ensuring that each image you use adds value to the learner experience, which again increases white space, making a better overall design for everyone.

Screen readers will not function well with Adobe Flash. Flash is continuous movement or animation, so it doesn't easily lend itself to alt text. You'd have to have paragraphs of content explaining the interaction. Avoiding Flash when possible will be in the best interest of your learners. Flash is also deprecated in new web browsers and will likely need to be changed in the future.

Magnification allows learners to zoom in on a certain part of the screen. One of the biggest complaints learners have when using magnification is animation on a small portion of the screen. If, on the previous slide, you had the navigation button on the lower-right side of the screen and the learner had to magnify that area to click it, and then on the following screen, content started animating on the slide on the left side of the screen, they might miss it completely by the time they found what was happening. Whenever possible, have the learner perform some action before critical content leaves the screen. Using the new supervisor training example of having a difficult conversation, if learners need to read what the first person is saying to understand and respond, don't let that animation leave until they click to advance or click on the other character to start talking.

To that end, making the navigation consistent within the module will make it much easier for learners to navigate through the course. Ideally it will be consistent across all courses, but at a minimum each course is best practice.

Voice-over on slides will be a benefit to learners who are visually impaired. Allow them to choose when to advance the screen, particularly if (and hopefully it is) the content shown on the slide is unique from the spoken content.

Here again the supervisor training may have staff members with visual impairments. Designing for mobile first and using the best practices of adult learning will optimize the content for all learners.

Auditory Impairments

Fifteen percent of American adults, or approximately 37.5 million people, report that they have some trouble hearing (National Center for Health Statistics 2014). However, that shouldn't stop you from including sound in your modules. Here are some considerations you'll want to keep in mind with development.

A closed captioning button will allow learners to turn on text that is synchronized with the audio so they can follow along or read the content being spoken. Even learners without difficulty hearing will appreciate this if they're in a location where it isn't feasible for them to have sound. When there are multiple speakers in a presentation, consider changing the color or formatting of the text between the speakers to help learners understand that it's not one continuous train of thought from a single individual.

Think about the last time you watched a foreign film that had subtitles. How much of what was happening onscreen were you able to catch? If you can hear, you had background noise, tone of voice, and the ability to differentiate between the characters' voices to help you contextualize what you were reading. If your learners have auditory impairments, they may find themselves reading blocks of text and seeing that something is happening above, but not be able to process everything at once.

Consider our discussion in chapter 9 on lowering the cognitive load. In this situation, you aren't, so you need to consider adding space between changes. Having a button to advance the conversation, as discussed earlier with visual impairments, will also benefit learners with auditory impairments.

Most authoring tools include embedded closed captioning in the timeline to allow you to synchronize it. As with visual impairments, using Flash can pose a problem with closed captioning. Unless it's embedded into the timeline, it can be incredibly hard to synchronize captioning with the movie.

While music can be enjoyable, it can make it harder to differentiate between the sounds of the content and the background. Giving learners the option to turn music off can ameliorate this issue.

The same goes for the supervisor training with audio as it did with video. Using the best practices of adult learning will make it accessible to everyone.

Learning Disabilities

Many of the recommendations provided for visual and auditory impairments will benefit your learners with learning disabilities. Having the ability to turn on and off sound, giving them the opportunity to process each piece of content before it advances, and developing high-contrast, vector imagery will all be beneficial.

Individuals with learning disabilities will also greatly benefit from adaptive learning. If they have the opportunity to make lots of choices and receive individualized feedback in a low-pressure environment, they will be more likely to internalize and understand the context of the content and be able to produce the desired behavior changes more quickly.

For the supervisor training for staff with learning disabilities, consider what has been discussed so far with development. Ensuring the language level of the content meets the needs of the audience, simplifying the visuals for clarity of content, and offering closed captioning are all adult learning best practices and applicable for these learners.

What's Realistic?

As a department of one, you need to be realistic about what you can do with the time and money you have. There are a few things that are deal breakers in accessibility development:

- **Government entity or contractor:** 508 compliance is the law. You have to do it.
- **You know the demographics of your office and their accessibility requirements:** It might seem hard when you start development, but knowing that staff can actually use the training program you make is a wonderful feeling. It will make you a better developer in the long run because it's not done by everyone.
- **You've been told to do it:** Your organization is working for social justice and equality and wants to ensure that they already follow best practices so that if any employee joins who has an accessibility need, you've already met it.

Yes, it can be time consuming. Yes, it can seem like tons of work for a few people. It's worth it. There are a few hacks to help make your life easier.

Hack 1: Closed captioning generally takes four to six hours of time per hour of video. The most painful part of this is that you spend time transcribing all the raw footage to work with your SMEs to determine what to keep and what to scrap. To save some time, and lots of heartache, consider these tricks:

- **Free with YouTube pro account!** Use YouTube for transcribing your videos. Even if you won't ultimately house your videos there, you can upload your videos to YouTube (on a private channel if you don't want anyone to see them) and they will do basic transcription. You can download this into a number of files that you can use in your video editing software, in your e-learning authoring tool, or to send out for interpretation. YouTube will also subtitle in a multitude of additional languages. To be safe, you should still consider having a native speaker check this before deploying it to your audience.

- **Free!** If you've stuck to the storyboard, the script should be almost identical to what you've already written, so it's just a matter of copying and pasting the phrases onto the video.
- **Free!** Ask someone else in the office who's interested in e-learning if they'd like to help out. I've worked with receptionists and admin assistants who will transcribe. The caveat here is that when they get "real work," this can fall by the wayside. It's also not a good idea for long projects because they get bored and move on to something more exciting after the first few hours.
- **Low cost!** Hire transcription services. As of 2018, there are companies doing this for between 10 cents and a dollar a minute.

Hack 2: If you've ever taken training on your mobile device, you know how minimalistic the content is because of the screen. If you know that the majority of your learners are going to be taking training on their mobile devices, you will be developing for not only the most common use case, but also with best practices for accessibility. By developing for mobile, you're ensuring the value of each piece of content that you're adding.

Hack 3: Duplicate slides that have the alt text on them and make changes to keep from typing in the same content over and over. In several e-learning authoring tools, you can also save the alt text to the library, so that when you pull the same image again, it already comes with the alt text.

Legal Requirements

Often, your accessibility decisions might be requirements based on government regulation. While it can add extra time and work to projects, ultimately you'll be creating e-learning that can best fit the needs of all learners. The laws that are most commonly referenced for accessibility in the United States are Section 508 standards and Section 255 guidelines.

Voluntary consensus has been developed into the Web Content Accessibility Guidelines (WCAG) 2.0. Generally, this guidance states that technology needs to address the needs of individuals with "disabilities impacting vision, hearing, color perception, speech, cognition, manual dexterity, reach, and strength."

As of January 11, 2018, government entities and contractors must abide by the updated regulations for all future development. Content developed before 2018 is called "safe harbor" and does not have to be updated until the content is altered.

Information specific to e-learning and 508 compliance is available online. Interestingly, the context behind this legislation is that if e-learning were developed with the fundamentals of adult learning principles, it would meet the 508 compliance requirements, so they're simply requiring that any e-learning purchased or developed be appropriate for an adult audience. Underpinning the legislation is Conrad Gottfredson's work on ensuring effective content and evaluating its instructional integrity. It includes additional information on how to source content that meets the 508 standards and what to do if it is not commercially available.

The section 508 government website (www.section508.gov) details more information about this legislation and preferred vendors for helping you with your development of compliant materials. This website provides guidance on how to create accessible products and has a test for accessibility. Unfortunately, the test for accessibility in 2018 only includes websites. For more information about 508 compliance and what it means for you, this website also includes a library of online training programs, several of which offer certificates or continuous learning points.

If you happen to work for a multinational company or one outside the United States, you'll also need to be aware of accessibility regulations there. The previous discussion focused on developing in the United States, but similar legislation is required for development in the European Union and

Australia. Canada is in the process of implementing new standards that will be required by 2025, known as the Federal Accessibility Act. Several provinces already have legislation in place.

Again, while your organization may not currently be required to meet these guidelines, implementing them now will ensure you're developing higher-quality content that is accessible to a wider audience.

Next

When you're comfortable that your content is accessible, it's time to share it with your SMEs and a group of testers, and launch it to the target audience.

CHAPTER 12

Testing and Sharing

Your module is done! You've analyzed, designed, and developed. Now you are ready to roll it out. To ensure a smooth implementation, here are a few steps to follow before submitting the content to the learners.

Alpha Test With SMEs

The module is complete, and it works on your computer. Who better to be the first-round tester for your content than your group of subject matter experts? The alpha, or first, test of your content should be sharing it with the SMEs to ensure that it is what they expected and works the way they think it should.

Don't worry about finishing all modules in a course before sending them for alpha testing. Instead, you can send them as they are developed. Just be sure to post your module where it can be reviewed on multiple devices. You can do this through your LMS and use version control for updates, or post it elsewhere.

Generally, this round goes fairly quickly. Because you've had the SMEs sign off on all the rounds of storyboard, nothing should be a surprise. They'll be happy, maybe have minor changes, and tell you to move to beta (second-round) testing.

With the new supervisor training example, you're likely to have a number of SMEs who offer content on the various parts of supervision. If they haven't taken the full course prior to this point, ask them to take all the parts of it to ensure the usability and cohesiveness of everything together, as learners will experience it. If this is the first time they are seeing the other parts, it will be important to emphasize that you do not want content changes. If an egregious issue arises, you will want to involve the project sponsor to mediate if the change suggested by one SME on another SME's content is valid. However, if you've developed in a cohesive, transparent environment, the likelihood of deal-breaker changes at this phase are minimal.

Embracing the Reality

After completing a module, I sent it to one of the SMEs for the first round of testing. It was a long compliance module with lots of integrated videos and animations. After about 10 minutes, I received a phone call that the SME was stuck on slide 5 (I put in the slide numbers during testing to help me resolve issues). After a few minutes of back and forth, I asked about the tech in use. The SME was on her personal cell phone using data to view the module! After she realized the training module wasn't designed to be taken on a mobile device, she tested it on her office computer with a Wi-Fi connection. She called me the next day to say it all worked perfectly.

Be very clear what devices you're supporting and how from the beginning. If you are supporting computers, tablets, and mobile devices, consider how to design storyboards for the differences in consumption.

Beta Test for Quality Control

Now it's time to find out where the whole course doesn't work. Hopefully you have access to the supported devices that your learners are expected to use when taking courses. This can be several types of mobile phones, tablets, and computers, as well as a variety of browsers. In a perfect world, you are not the person who is doing the testing. There are two reasons for this:

1. You've seen this content so many times that you're blind to some errors, like typos.

2. You know what you expect users to do, and you need them to do the wonderfully unexpected things that they actually do to know if they can get through the module or not.

Setting up a lottery where learners can win the chance to be the beta testers of your content can be a fun and engaging way to find an audience to check your module.

It is important to work with the HR department to determine if the beta testers can earn credit for course completion during beta testing. If someone is on the supervisory track, they will be an optimal candidate for beta testing, but if they don't get credit for taking the course and have to take it twice, it may sour their overall opinion of the process and training. In that case, work with people who are interested in supporting your development, but aren't as invested in the content right now.

Advice From the Trenches: Hadiya Nuriddin

Regardless of the size of your learning and development department, we all face similar challenges when it comes to quality control and assurance. We all want to release perfect materials and modules, but there is rarely enough time and resources available to ensure that happens. There is no easy answer—you can't manufacture more time, get your company to hire a dedicated resource, or simply create flawless materials just because you want to.

Whether you're a team of one or one hundred, if you have no quality control team, the only answer is to build a formal process that you can manage by yourself. This process needs to have it all: goals, standards, steps, definitions, responsibilities, and most of all, flexibility. Adding this process to your project plans may give you justification for pushing back on unreasonable deadlines. A formalized process also opens possibilities for you to teach other people throughout the company how to play a role. For example, if you have a process for how to conduct a review, create a job aid and use it to train the receptionist or an intern.

Your work flow can also include many of the software and online tools used in other industries that may make your process easier. Every quality control process will likely need three types of tools: a tracking system for documenting and communicating errors, a testing system for identifying errors (in this case, the system may only be a strategy for finding errors), and a storage system for storing and sharing documents and courses. There are no perfect tools, but keep trying until you find the right combination. But a process is only useful if it's usable, so do not overengineer it by adding tools just because you can.

Implementing a quality control process is a challenge for most industries that create products. The problem with learning and development is that we do not view the materials we create as products, so quality control is an afterthought. That does not have to be true for you, however. Nothing is stopping you from creating a formalized process for yourself or your team. The bottom line is that quality checks are going to happen—either you are going to make time to do it as part of your process or your clients and learners will do it as they take the course. In other words, you'll pay now or pay later.

Whether you're working by yourself or with your team, there are two types of quality control, or QC, that you need to run. The first is usability. You need to know that someone can get through the course. You want them to take it as if they're actually taking it and see how they do. This is where having current employees in a lottery-style situation works well. Hopefully your course does work well, testers act like you expect them to, and they get through it. They can give you feedback on weird things that happen, but they still take the whole thing and earn credit.

The second is harder; it's where you try to break it. When I am asked to do QC for other people, this is the one that I think is fun. When doing it for myself, there is usually some crying involved.

When trying to break the course, encourage your testers to click the forward button over and over, click every button on the screen multiple times, click on a character when another character is speaking, or—if they can—advance the slide without watching an entire video by pausing the course. In essence, they are aiming to be your worst-nightmare learner. They're mimicking, for example, someone who doesn't want to take this course because the content is "stupid" or "a waste of my time" and is trying to click enough to earn the points or get to the test and then Google the answers to get credit with the minimal amount of work.

Embracing the Reality: Nikki O'Keeffe

The review stage is crucial. When you are working as an e-learning team of one, you may be the only person spending hours and hours designing, developing, editing, and publishing your course. It can be easy to miss little details, such as typos, broken links, missing triggers, or narration that is timed incorrectly.

As a result, have someone else try to "break" your course during the review process. If you fail to get another set of eyes on your e-learning courses during the review stage, your learners could be the ones to discover any embarrassing errors. The publishing, uploading, and LMS launch process can be cumbersome depending on your organization, so you may not be able to resolve errors quickly once your course is live. And it is always best to catch issues *before* learners call out your mistakes on the day your course is pushed out to the LMS.

For instance, one course I developed on communicating with clients ended up having a spelling error in the answer to a fill-in-the-blank question. Spelling errors happen, right? No big deal? Wrong. The impact of the spelling error meant that not a single learner was able to receive credit for the mandatory training that required a 100 percent passing score. (And an influx of emails to my inbox of learners asking for assistance!)

Now, you're probably thinking that you don't really want to fix the issues you might find doing this. No person in their right mind is going to click all three of the voice boxes on the screen at the same time to make the conversation completely unintelligible. Well, they might do that by accident, and if they do, can they still listen to each one in sequence again? Or if they listen to the scenario out of order, can they reset it to get it in the correct order?

Ideally, you'll also provide them with different devices on which to take the training course and have at least two people per device, so that you can determine if it was a replicable error on the test or not.

Personally, this is my least favorite part of development. I hate editing the work that I've done, particularly after it's "all done." This is where my projects will get stuck in the hopper for a long time, because I know there are lots of little errors that have been submitted to me, and I now have to make time to actually make the changes. Don't get stuck here. It's not done until learners have tested it. This is a critically important step in implementation.

Getting Feedback From the Alpha and Beta

To facilitate the data collection from your testing rounds, provide testers with the final storyboard, or a data sheet like the storyboard, with the number of the slide on both the form and on the screen. Note to testers that it will be removed for the final publication and is there to facilitate their ability to provide feedback on where the errors are occurring. It can be helpful to walk through an example with them of the kinds of feedback you would like to receive. You don't want an essay per item, but you need to know when things are occurring that are unexpected or nonfunctional. Don't let your testers feel like they spent a lot of time giving you feedback that you didn't use. Conversely, don't have them take it and then not give you actionable feedback for your final publication.

Ensure that the form includes their name, the date they tested each part, and the device and browser used in testing. Consider the example in Figure 12-1.

A chart like this gives testers the ability to take notes and see what the expected interactions are on each slide and what should happen based on making choices. It's important for them to know that you want them to test every possible path, particularly in a branching scenario, regardless of how unlikely it is, to ensure that it works. If they clicked the right answer and got negative feedback, you need to know that you've made a coding error.

Figure 12-1. Testing Feedback Job Aid

Slide Number	Onscreen Graphics	Audio	Interactions	Other Feedback
1001	Man on left Woman on right Speech bubble animates over man	Man's voice, 30 seconds	Click on woman to continue	
1002	Man on left Woman on right Speech bubble animates over woman	Woman's voice, 10 seconds	Click on man to continue	
1003	Man on left 3 choices to select	Question read in man's voice	Coach pops up with thought bubble Answer 1- 1004 Answer 2- 1005 Answer 3- 1006	
1004	Woman frowning, pop-up message with 3 choices	Woman's voice, 40 seconds	Coach pops up with thought bubble Answer 1- 1007 Answer 2- 1008 Answer 3- 1009	

Publishing

Once you've resolved any remaining errors across the variety of devices, it's time to post it and share the course with your learners.

When adding the course to an LMS, you can aggregate multiple modules together to make a program, or you can build in precursor courses before this one can be taken. You may even automatically assign the course to learners based on certain parameters, such as entering a certain training series or earning a certain amount of skill points to become eligible for the course. Consider meeting with your SMEs to ask them questions about the desired accessibility of the module:

- What is the minimum requirement to access this content?
- Can anyone who meets the minimum requirements access this content, or do they need another step or approval?

- Can learners take the content in any order?
- When the content is complete, what happens? Who is notified? What must learners do to earn final credit?
- What should learners take after this course?
- Is this course a precursor to another course?
- What happens if a learner is unable to pass a certain portion of the course?

Once it's loaded and you can see it in the appropriate locations, you'll want to verify that you can see it and it opens. From there, take the course on the device that you expect most of the audience to use. Ensure that the functionality meets your expectations.

Verify that the results show up in the LMS, and that those results match the results within the module itself. When they do, you're all set to share the course with learners.

Finally, ensure that you've added a place for feedback from the learners. At a minimum, create a generic Likert scale that can be used for all training to understand and compare what learners like and do not and the applicability of content.

Next

As an e-learning department of one, you might consider the rollout to be the end of the project—after all, it's now on the manager to ensure that performance changes. However, no e-learning project is complete without follow-up on your part to assess and evaluate its effectiveness.

CHAPTER 13

Assessment and Evaluation

Now that the module is published and the learners are taking it, you can begin the assessment and evaluation process. The main question is: Did the training program solve the underlying problem that it was created to address?

To answer this question, you first need to grasp the difference between assessment and evaluation. Assessment is how you determine if learners understand the content. This is why you would, for example, give a test at the end of a training program. Evaluation is how you determine if the training program is effective. It incorporates the assessment scores, learner feedback, and business outcomes, among other elements.

Several different evaluation methods are generally accepted in the industry, including the Kirkpatrick Model. This model has four levels; they increase in implementation difficulty, but offer increasing rewards of data.

Evaluation Levels

The first level, Reaction, can be implemented easily today. It can be as simple as a Likert scale or smile sheet (Figure 13-1). If you don't have an LMS that will allow you to set it up, you can use survey software or Google Forms.

Figure 13-1. Level 1 Evaluation

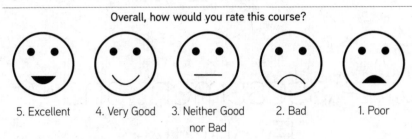

The problem with this evaluation is that it simply tells you whether learners enjoyed the class, and not whether it was effective at meeting the objective. Recently there has been a movement toward using a performance-based Likert scale, making it related to the content of the course while still using the same easy to implement scale. Sample scale items include:

- As a result of this course:
  » I have obtained the necessary skills to become a supervisor.
  » I am comfortable having a conversation with a direct report about timeliness.
  » I am comfortable conducting a performance review with a direct report.

You could continue to use the five-point strongly agree to strongly disagree scale to easily aggregate the data.

This update to the level one questions feeds nicely into Kirkpatrick Level 2, Learning. This is similar to the types of assessments you would be familiar with from school, such as chapter or unit tests.

If you've used the performance-based Likert scale in Level 1, now you know the perceived comfort level with the content. You can validate that by asking specific topical questions. For ease of development, many e-learning authoring tools will provide you with questions that are easy to grade, such as multiple choice, true or false, matching, sequencing, and short answer. Examples of these questions are:

- Our corporate management philosophy is: (Select the best answer)
- We conduct performance reviews with our staff every week. (True or False)
- Management values are _____, open communication, and integrity. (Fill in the blank)

If, like many learners, summative exams make you nervous, with flash-backs to grade school, you're in luck. Scenario-based learning assesses learners in a less high-pressure way and facilitates reteaching. Embedding realistic work examples allows the learner to go through a simulated world and make decisions. These decisions are mini assessments where coaching can be offered through support and feedback.

Advice From the Trenches

Recently I developed a compliance module that all staff had to take annually. Working with the SME, we researched the underpinnings of the annual requirement; it turned out that the only thing required annually was ensuring the staff were comfortable enough with the content to be able to act accordingly with standards.

The SME and I devised a path for staff who had been with the company for more than a year, so they would have taken the full course at least once. When they opened the module, they were allowed to decide between testing out of the content or taking the full module and then the test. If they did not earn a perfect score on the test when testing out, they were automatically pushed to the full module. If they took the full module and didn't earn a perfect score, they were offered scaffolded answers and allowed to retake it until they did.

The drawback to developing an embedded assessment is that it is most easily tracked with xAPI. Most LMSs support SCORM, but xAPI is limited to a small subset. You can code your way around this using JavaScript and custom points, or enlist a member of the IT team.

However, this can add time to your development, and you need to weigh it against the potential gains.

The benefits to embedded scenarios using xAPI is that they can help you evaluate at Kirkpatrick Level 3, Behavior. Using xAPI, you can enable things outside the training bubble to count toward the work that learners do. Each time their supervisor observes them doing their on-the-job work correctly based on the training course, they can add information to the LRS and about the learners' overall understanding of the training content.

Finally, the fourth level of the Kirkpatrick Model is Results. At the end of the process, when reviewing the content, ask:

- Has our situation changed?
- Are learners acting differently?

This is where you can truly assess if your training has achieved the original objective. The learners attended the training course, understood the content, internalized it, and made behavior changes. Now, you're able to observe and appreciate the results.

If after the content development and deployment the situation has not changed and you're sure the learners are taking and understanding the module, you will want to consider if something else needs to happen at the organization to support the change. This generally becomes an operational discussion to enforce requested changes.

Start small with your assessment. If you've never run assessments of your staff before, consider doing Level 1 and Level 2. Build up to Levels 3 and 4 as your organization becomes more familiar with your modules and the value of the information you gather from these assessments.

Many people have found that the scores on the assessments are lower than they would like, particularly when learners are assessed several days after the original training. To combat the forgetting curve, where the amount of knowledge retained drops off immediately following training, some developers have implemented spaced learning, which spreads out the content and reinforces it for the learners.

Spaced Learning

Have you ever attended a training course and at the end of it thought, "That was phenomenal—I am going to change the way I do this work and it's going to be so much better"? Yet a month later, you barely remember that you went to a training course, and never implemented any of the information back on the job. Research done in the 1890s by psychologist Hermann Ebbinghaus shows that you start to forget the second you leave the room; from there, memory drops off exponentially. Called the forgetting curve, the concept basically shows that no single training course is going to stick with an employee after a matter of a few days.

More recent studies have attempted to eliminate or reduce the forgetting curve. Several companies specialize in contacting employees on very specific timeframes following a training course and asking the right types of questions to ensure that recall of training content stays around 80 percent.

Advice From the Trenches

You don't have to do anything particularly technical to set up spaced learning. My organization offers a new supervisor training week. Each department comes in and presents roughly 30 minutes of content to the new supervisors so they know the primary person in each department they can contact for assistance. We found that these supervisors weren't able to recall whom they'd met or why they'd contact them, even with a binder full of notes and handouts. We instituted a drip email campaign. At the end of each day, an email with a link to a short video went out discussing one of the content pieces from that day. A week later, we sent another email with a flow chart. Two days after that, they received another email with a pull quote.

We managed the whole process through Microsoft Outlook using the delay delivery feature. At the end of the month, we sent out a survey asking the attendees how they felt about the "boost" series. Several respondents said they'd forgotten about particular presentations and were reminded about them. Consequently, they went back to their binders because they recalled other information as a result of these boosts.

We have elected to continue doing this through email for our management series until we have a full year of results, and will then come up with another option for our online training for all staff.

There are a number of ways that you can implement spaced learning. One of the most effective is to minimize binge e-learning. Taking courses back-to-back doesn't allow learners the time they need to process the content. Forcing a gap between when learners can take the subsequent module requires them to wait to add to the information they've obtained. Now, while they're waiting for the new information, you can offer opportunities for repetition. They could retake the original module or take microlearning or tests related to the content. Repetition is key to ensuring that they remember the content.

Starting the next lesson without reviewing the previous lesson will cause learners to pull from their long-term memory to make any required associations to build upon the content.

Avoiding Analysis Paralysis

To gather data, you'll pull it from your LMS or the website where you host the organization's e-learning modules. If that isn't an option at this point, consider requesting it as funds become available to help you know more about your learners and the value of the modules you create.

The amazing and horrible thing about assessments and other data collection methods is the deluge of results that you'll receive. Even with just Levels 1 and 2, you're talking an average of 10 questions each, per assessment, per person! It can add up quickly. If you add in the results from xAPI on top of that, you've got potentially hundreds of touchpoints. It can get overwhelming—fast.

Take a deep breath and relax. Gather the information for when you need it and you have time to wrap your head around it. Better to collect data you aren't using than not.

At the beginning of each month, run a report on module usage and the number of times it takes for staff to pass them.

If you find that some of your courses take learners several times to pass, you may want to consider watching a new learner take the course to discover usability errors or gaps in content. Ask learners who have already completed the course if they had questions that could be better addressed in updates. Particularly as you update content or create another level for an existing training course, look at the data you've collected and assess how effective the current course is at meeting the needs of the individual and the organization.

Think of results like email. You don't want to have a dashboard running in the background all the time because it will distract you from the work that you need to be doing. However, you need to check it every so often to ensure that you're dealing with the issues that arise.

Evaluating Yourself

Many new e-learning developers—or any learning and development professional for that matter—get caught up in evaluating their programs at the expense of evaluating their own performance. How do you feel about what you've developed? Knowing that you have limitations on time and resources, are you proud of your creation? Did you meet your, and others, expectations?

In reviewing a module that you've completed, did you:
- Try something new?
- Use best practices in design?
- Design a level of interactivity that makes it e-learning and not talking at someone?

Is this module something you'd show your parents? Is it something you'd submit for comments from other e-learning developers? Would you be willing to enter it into a contest? If not, think about why you wouldn't and what would need to happen in your future module development for you to be proud enough of it to submit it to win an e-learning award.

To get better, you need to continually experience what other developers are doing and share what you're doing to get feedback. Consider your professional development an important aspect of the development process. You need to grow as a developer to ensure that you're offering your learners the best module that you can with what you have.

Next

Building on self-evaluation and continuous growth, the next and final chapter covers options to further your professional development. Just because you're working on your own doesn't mean you should allow the never-ending work to get in the way of becoming better at your job by learning new skills. Chapter 14 gives you a place to start.

CHAPTER 14

Resources and Professional Development

Particularly when you're working alone as an e-learning developer, it can be hard to maintain focus and excitement while developing new content. If you haven't experienced it already, you're bound to come across someone who looks scared or annoyed when you say, "I build online training, like what you've taken at work." Their reaction is usually followed by a story about the most boring hour of this person's life, usually spent taking a compliance course. When you've heard a few too many of these, you'll need to be inspired by the fascinating and wonderful e-learning training that does exist.

Focusing on Your Professional Development

Build in time for your professional development. Hopefully by reading this book you've been able to identify any knowledge gaps where you can focus your study. When you're working as a department of one, you may find yourself in a rut, developing the same type of training or the same activities over and over.

Using examples of projects that you find on the Internet or at conferences can help you make engaging and effective training. At least once a year, try to attend a major training conference. The networking opportunities and connections you build are immeasurably valuable whenever you're stuck and need someone to bounce an idea off of.

As mentioned in chapter 8, the Articulate community runs weekly challenges to allow developers to show off their skills. If you don't have time to do weekly challenges, make a point to review the examples that other developers provide. These are also useful for showing potential ideas to SMEs for something that you could develop using your own content. Additionally, subscribe to and read several blogs, but don't focus solely on ones about e-learning authoring tools. You can get great ideas even from development done through other platforms.

Advice From the Trenches: Nikki O'Keeffe

Find a mentor to learn from. For example, watching someone navigate in an authoring tool will give you a fresh perspective. You may think you are doing a task the fastest and most creative way, and then you see someone else do it a different way. E-learning can be frustrating. There will be times when you get stuck and it will be beneficial to have someone to reach out to and say, "Hey, what am I doing wrong here?"

Get basic training to start, otherwise the process can feel intimidating. Learn by doing; try playing around with the authoring tool. Read about the principles of proper instructional design for e-learning, and what entails so-called improper e-learning instructional design, such as a slide with text, another slide with more content, and then a quiz. It's about user interaction, challenges, and problem solving. It is one thing to know how to use an authoring tool. It is another thing to create powerful e-learning that affects behavior changes on the job.

There are tons of free resources out there to help you. Use them! You are not alone even though it might feel that way. Webcasts, webinars, communities, templates, ideas, and how-to videos are all a good place to start. Many other developers out there are self-taught departments of one, who may have similar struggles and successes that you are having.

Remember:
- E-learning is training and should be treated as such.
- Resource your project wisely.
- Don't make your learners review your course.
- File management is key to long-term success.
- Reach out for help.
- Authoring tool expertise is not enough.
- Resources are abundant if you look for them.

Optimizing Time and Resources as a Department of One

Just because you're in an environment with limited resources doesn't mean that you can't have tools and support from your organization. Here are some tools, software titles, and other resources that you can look for within the organization to use or repurpose in your department:

- Communicating With SMEs and Learners
  - » SharePoint
  - » Microsoft Project
  - » Microsoft Outlook
  - » Project management software (Jira)
  - » Bug-tracking software (Bugzilla)
- Instructional Design Knowledge and Tools
  - » WebEx, GoToMeeting, and Adobe Presenter
  - » Company contracts
  - » Adobe Form Creator
- Development Tools
  - » Adobe Creative Suite
  - » Microsoft Office
  - » Audacity
- Project Management Knowledge and Tools

- » Project management software (Jira)
- » Policies and procedures for project completion
- » Stakeholder register
- » Tech support ticketing system
- » Bug-tracking software (Bugzilla)
- Graphics, Audio, and Video
  - » Style guide
  - » Resource library
  - » Graphic designer

This is a combination of what I found within my organization and what I purchase to support my e-learning development. Figure 14-1 maps out how the different types of tools align with different stages of e-learning creation.

Figure 14-1. How Certain Tools Align With the Development Process

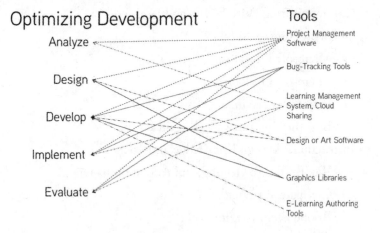

As a developer of learning, you're likely to believe in continuous improvement and professional development. Because you bought this book, you're likely looking to lessen your skills gaps and enhance your strengths. You'll want to build in time for increasing your knowledge and keeping up with

best practices. If the only exposure you have to e-learning is what you've created yourself, you're limited to what you can come up with and what you know. Spend some time looking at what is available from competitors and ATD, as well as professional examples from your e-learning authoring tools. You may also consider developing content for challenge programs and contests to expand your skill set.

New organizations, conferences, and programs are thought up and shared by brilliant people every day. As of this writing, these are the ones that have stood the test of time and will hopefully be there when you're ready to find them. Please also ask other professionals for their advice for newer information.

Professional Organizations and Their Conferences

Here are some great resources for e-learning:

- **Association for Talent Development (ATD, www.td.org).** I would recommend joining this organization. They offer tons of classes, publish books (like this one), and have several conferences annually. In particular, if you're looking for an entry-level course, the ATD Essentials Series covers a variety of topics in training and development. ATD also has one of the most widely recognized training credentials, the Certified Professional in Learning and Performance (CPLP) and the newer Associate Professional in Talent Development (APTD). Regional ATD chapters offer special interest groups (SIGs), like e-learning SIGs, where you can meet other professionals and learn about industry trends.
- **The eLearning Guild (www.elearningguild.com).** This organization is for e-learning developers. Best of all, their

entry-level membership is free, so you have nothing to lose by joining. The eLearning Guild holds my favorite conference, DevLearn, every fall. This conference brings together developers and vendors to discuss and train on cutting-edge technology.

- **eLearning Industry (https://elearningindustry.com).** Another e-learning-specific organization, this group provides my favorite newsletter and email blast content. You can receive a daily summary of their latest articles. They also regularly publish free e-books.

- *Training* **magazine (https://trainingmag.com).** *Training* magazine offers tons of webinars. They have at least one every day of the workweek. Their trainers are industry experts who cover a wide range of topics from graphic design to Kirkpatrick assessment to performance management. These are all free; if you can't attend them live they are available to watch on demand.

- **Training Industry (www.trainingindustry.com).** This organization has a subsection specifically curated for e-learning development. Sign up for their newsletter to get a stream of their latest and greatest content.

Advice From the Trenches

It's important to me to have a face-to-face connection with other e-learning developers. I make a point of prioritizing my time to allow me to attend one national conference every year. I also joined the local ATD chapter and attend the special interest group for e-learning to allow me to see what others are developing and to share our experiences. Since we spend so much time at computers, and even more working as departments of one, the connection with others will push you and keep you grounded.

And here are some more general resources I find valuable:

- *Chief Learning Officer* **magazine (www.clomedia.com).** If you're interested in becoming a chief learning officer (CLO) or just want more information about strategic learning development, the articles in this website and magazine will help you get a big-picture understanding of where your work fits into overall talent management and some ideas on how to show the value of your work.

- **Society for Human Resource Management (SHRM, www.shrm.org).** The trend in training is for us to be members of the HR department. SHRM is the most widely recognized HR networking and credentialing organization.

- **International Society for Performance Improvement (ISPI, www.ispi.org).** If the goal of training is to effect behavior change, the International Society for Performance Improvement is a wonderful resource for best practices and current research. Many instructional designers choose to become members of this organization.

- **Project Management Institute (PMI, www.pmi.org).** If you want an organization that is well run, highly structured, and provides and requires continuous learning, it's hard to find one better than the Project Management Institute. You can obtain numerous credentials on various aspects of project management. PMI requires at least 30 hours of training in project management every three years for a person to maintain their certification.

While many of the websites I've listed have newsletters and will email you daily, there are a few blogs that are also worth space in your inbox:

- **The Rapid E-Learning Blog by Tom Kuhlmann of Articulate (http://blogs.articulate.com/rapid-elearning).** In addition to the community challenges (mentioned in the next section), this blog provides tons of tips, tricks, and freebies. You don't have to use Articulate to take advantage of the tools provided.

- **Experience E-Learning by Christy Tucker (https:// christytucker.wordpress.com).** This blog focuses on the development of instructional design skills and tips. Check out the visitor's guide to understand the work that she's doing and see examples in her portfolio.
- **Cathy Moore's Let's Save the World From Boring Training (http://blog.cathy-moore.com).** If you're interested in action mapping, Cathy Moore is the ultimate resource. In addition to her newsletter, she also shares e-learning samples: http://blog.cathy -moore.com/resources/elearning-samples.

Advice and Sharing

A fun place to test your skills is the Articulate community challenges: https://community.articulate.com/hubs/e-learning-challenges. You do not have to use Articulate products to author the modules in this challenge, making it accessible to everyone. You can review and submit to all of the previous challenges in addition to competing in the weekly new ones.

LinkedIn may have started as a professional networking site, but it has a groups section that is also useful for asking work-related questions.

Summary

Working in a department of one can be a wonderful thing. You can be inspired by projects that you see other developers make and you can learn how to build them for your organization. You can study the effects of different types of e-learning on your learners and determine the most effective way to teach any concept that they need to learn.

Seek out e-learning developers and share your products with them. Get inspiration, support, and feedback from our wonderful community. You'll find that we're a passionate group of people who want to share our knowledge and experiences with everyone who joins us in the field. While you are a department of one, there are many of us, and more every year as we become freelancers and contractors.

Welcome. We're happy you're here.

Acknowledgments

To all the "departments of one," I thank you for sharing your knowledge and expertise with the rest of us. For burning the midnight oil to be better developers and find the right solution for our audiences. For building e-learning for an organization that wouldn't be able to have it if you didn't wear the many hats required of a person to be alone, supporting an organization.

Thank you, Jack Harlow, for the many rounds of edits and meetings we had over the course of this book's conception. I absolutely could not have done it without you. Thank you, Justin Brusino, for meeting with me and going on the journey to write this book with ATD. Thank you, Susan Kaiden, for hearing my initial pitch on this topic and connecting me with Justin. Thank you, Caroline Coppel, for your copyediting expertise.

Thank you to all the experts who contributed to this book. You've inspired me so much and I am incredibly thankful for your willingness to share your expertise on this subject.

Thank you to all of the ATD Essentials Series trainers whose courses helped me improve and extend my own training development.

Ellen Lees, thank you for being the best supervisor I've ever had, for inspiring me to go to graduate school, and for sitting through countless hours of thesis videos.

Thank you, Shawn Lowrie and Eva Murphy, for being the first audience I had for e-learning and helping me develop better training.

Cordelia Fallon, thank you for listening to me read chapters of this book to you as you knit for our company project.

Brian Schmedinghoff, thank you for editing and providing feedback on many chapters of work and for helping me process each step in its due course.

Thank you, Mika Yoshida, for introducing me to many new and wonderful experiences and for your continuous support.

Thank you, Jonathan Tessero, for being an inspiration for the way that you live your life. I am thankful every day to get to speak with you and for your guidance.

Thank you, Christopher Vella, for being a rock in my life. Our friendship has weathered many years and will continue to do so.

Thank you, Mom, for taking me to years of meetings and conferences to allow me to follow my passion. Thank you, Dad, for sharing with me a love of learning about everything. Andrea, thank you for sharing my love of education and talking instructional theory with me. Thank you, Vanessa, for always supporting me, being the voice of my graduate thesis, and always putting a smile on my face.

References and Resources

References

ATD (Association for Talent Development). 2014. "ATD Competency Model." ATD. www.td.org/certification/atd-competency-model.

Defelice, R. 2018. "How Long to Develop One Hour of Training? Updated for 2017." ATD Insights, January 9. www.td.org/insights /how-long-does-it-take-to-develop-one-hour-of-training-updated -for-2017.

National Center for Health Statistics. 2014. "Summary Health Statistics for U.S. Adults: National Health Interview Survey, 2012." *Vital and Health Statistics*, Series 10, Number 260. Hyattsville, MD: U.S. Department of Health and Human Services.

NFB (National Federation of the Blind). 2018. "Statistical Facts About Blindness in the United States." NFB, June. https://nfb.org /blindness-statistics.

Resources

Accessibility

- Accessibility for E-Learning: Section 508 and WCAG: www
  .td.org/insights/accessibility-for-e-learning-section-508-and-wcag
- Essentials of Designing Accessible (508 Compliant) Programs and
  Materials: www.td.org/education-courses/essentials-of-designing
  -accessible-508-compliant-programs-and-materials
- Virginia's Checklist for E-Learning Accessibility: www.vadsa.org
  /ace/checklist.htm

Assessment and Evaluation

- Kirkpatrick Partners: www.kirkpatrickpartners.com/Our
  -Philosophy/The-Kirkpatrick-Model

Needs Assessment

- ATD Competency Model: www.td.org/certification
  /atd-competency-model
- ATD's Needs Assessment Certificate Program: www.td.org
  /education-courses/needs-assessment-certificate
- International Society for-Performance Improvement: www.ispi.org

About the Author

Emily's passion is sharing knowledge with learners on any topic. It started at an early age, when she would help her father build presentations for his medical conferences. One of her favorite games to play as a child was "Respi-baby"—a simulation game for neonatologists on infant respiration therapy. Her dad liked to joke that if his 10-year-old could save the babies, the medical students working for him should be able to as well.

Emily is one of the many e-learning developers who found herself doing this job by taking on another project on a completely different career path. Originally she planned on working in market research and found herself creating marketing materials with instructional videos. During that time, she earned a master's degree in instructional science and technology at night. She then went on to work for the federal government, a startup, a museum, and several nonprofit organizations.

She enjoys working with animals, having volunteered in equine- and dog-assisted therapy. She is a classical bassist and has performed in several community orchestras and musicals. She travels extensively and tries to learn about the languages and cultures wherever she goes. Emily has enjoyed living all over the United States. She spent her childhood moving progressively eastward. As an adult, she's been discovering the U.S. coasts. She resides in Portland, Oregon, with her lab, George.

You can learn more about her projects at www.idemily.com.

Index

In this index, *f* denotes figure and *t* denotes table.

T

talent, amateur, 113–115, 114*t*
technical teams, 40
technology, 4, 8, 66
testing
    activities, 97–98
    alpha test with SMEs, 147–148
    beta test quality control, 4, 23, 148–152, 153*f*
    feedback from alpha and beta, 152, 153*f*
    storyboarding, 82–83
text-to-speech, 110–112
timeline, 27, 35–36, 52, 129–130
time/resources, optimizing, 165–167, 166*f*
training, existing, 8–11
Training Industry, 168
Training magazine, 168
transcribing videos, 143–144
transformative learning, 63–64

U

usability testing, 150

V

video
    about, 123, 123*f*, 127
    asset management, 43
    cartoon animations, 131
    Internet, 130–131
    planning for recording, 133–135
    post-production, 135–136
    recording own video, 128–129
    scripts, writing, 132–133
    timeline, 129–130
    whiteboard animations, 131–132
virtual reality, 61, 68
visual impairments, 138–141
voice-over. *See* audio

W

waterfall model. *See* ADDIE model
webinars, 56–57, 67–68
websites, 67, 107

X

xAPI, 103–104, 157–158

Y

YouTube pro account, 143–144